MY COLOURFUL WORLD OF POETRY

S R SUTTON

WORKBOOK PRESS LLC
187 E Warm Springs Rd,
Suite B285 Las Vegas NV 89119 USA

Website: https://workbookpress.com/
Hotline: 1-888-818-4856
Email: admin@workbookpress.com

Ordering Information:

Quantity sales. Special discounts are available on quantity purchases by corporations, associations, and others. For details, contact the publisher at the address above.

Library of Congress Control Number:

ISBN-13:   978-1-963718-05-8 Paperback Version
              978-1-963718-06-5 Digital Version

REV. DATE: 02/15/2024

ABOUT THE BOOK

This book is a collection of my poetry over the years inspired by the life I have led, working in the care setting and travelling all over the world. I hope you enjoy my work and may find it useful to use in the right settings, for instance 'Those in grief' has been used in funerals. My life has been rather colourful to say the least and I have been in a few situations, facing danger and adventure bringing me to the present day. Now at sixty-five, I can reflect on this and laugh at the funny events and sigh with relief at actually surviving other situations. I consider each event as a blip in my life and nothing more, yes, I do have nightmare from my worst experiences as a teenager but I just thank God that I survived to tell the tale. These poems also reflect society as it is today around the world including hate crime, racism, sexism, homophobia and much more.

ABOUT THE AUTHOR

I am S R Sutton author of fantasy horror novels and poetry; I have spent years of my life perfecting this art and feel passionate about many causes. It is my aim to demonstrate to the world exactly how I feel about society today living in Manchester. I haven't always lived here; I grew up in Lichfield Staffordshire educated at Chadsmead infants and junior school and went on to Netherstowe where I developed my gift as an artist and appreciation of poetry.

I was a care assistant for sixteen years before going into further education and going to Salford university graduating in 1999 and becoming a qualified general nurse, I entered education again at Manchester university as a student mental health nurse. My writing skills developed from writing essays and I was soon able to produce novels such as cracked porcelain, Understanding Jodie and the Harrington curse under various names such as Sarah Ruth Scott and Simon Robert Sinclair with the initials SRS. I continued to write poetry from 1988 to the present 2021, writing five books of poetry including Manchester and beyond poems from Manchester, Life (as we know it) Deep in thought, out of the jar and the best of life the worst of life. My children Gemma, Jeni, Mike and Dan say they are proud of me, I respond by saying I do my best, this is what I tell everyone to just do your best. My appreciation for poetry came from my school days at Netherstowe thanks to my English teacher Miss Caines, she was also the head of the library back in the sixties and seventies a remarkable lady who looked as if she had stepped out of time from an earlier era judging by her hair style and the way she dressed.

Table of Contents

(I AM ME) SOPHIE
by Stephen Sutton

I am me; Sophie I am myself
All alone on my shelf
I want be my own identity
I want to live life totally free

This is the person
This is who I am
I could be a black sheep
Or a white fluffy lamb

But I am an individual
One of a kind
I know what I want
I know my own mind

So don't criticize me
Don't peck at my head
For I am not lazy
Waste life in my bed

I just want my freedom
To be left alone
Without hateful abuse
Please leave me on my own

S.O.P.H.I.E
by Stephen Sutton

Stamp out prejudice hatred
 And intolerance everywhere
Embrace individual thoughts
 And show them you care

Provide meaning and purpose
To those all around
Just because you are different
You are still sound

In memory of Sophie
Her name will live on
In a place in our hearts
We are as one

We fight for the right
The right to be me
As a free person
For all to see

The murder of Sophie Lancaster occurred in England in
August 2007 through hate crime

EVERY LIFE MATTERS
S R SUTTON

Treasure all creatures
Let's be kind
You will never know just
What you will find

Beneath the skin
Of men and women alike
Lives a certain person
That you may like

All you see is the make up
The image or camouflaged skin
A tattooed person
With dark clothes and so thin

Or maybe he is black, yellow or red
Fear not the colour that's in your head
For every life matters they count in the end
Live life in harmony just being a friend

Put aside every difference
Cast away all your hate
Welcome all nations
Before its too late

S.O.P.H.I.E

by Stephen Sutton

Stamp out prejudice hatred
 And intolerance everywhere
Embrace individual thoughts
 And show them you care

Provide meaning and purpose
To those all around
Just because you are different
You are still sound

In memory of Sophie
Her name will live on
In a place in our hearts
We are as one

We fight for the right
The right to be me
As a free person
For all to see

The murder of Sophie Lancaster occurred in England in
August 2007 through hate crime

So, end all hate crimes
Let peace lead you on
Love those who are different
Live life as one

HORRORS OF WAR

The cry of hunger
The moaning of pain
For here we are starving
Once again

Our bodies are thin
We feel very weak
With no one to help us
The future is bleak

The tears that we shed
Are common to me
If you want to see poverty
Then just look at me

The bloody battle still rages
With explosions all around
There is screaming and shouting
A horrific sound

Caught in a war
That we didn't need
Stop all this fighting
You hear us plead

HATED CRIMES

by Stephen Sutton

How can we justify hate for others?
When never even met
Do we remember being bullied?
So easy we forget

More hate crimes in the news
When will they end?
Do we call ourselves the guilty?
Never making friends

The victims lay before us
Kicked and in a state
Who is guilty for their beating?
Who do you even hate?

You tease the way they dress
You hate the way they speak
You hate the way they live their life
And when they turn the other cheek

Why can't you show them mercy?
Why can't this hatred end?
Why don't you just accept them?
And show them you're a friend

UNDERSTANDING JODIE

by Stephen Sutton

Jodie was a lovely girl
She wrote her journal well
She wrote about her teenage life
As if she lived in hell

Her sexuality was a problem
She never could understand
To live her life as a lesbian
Why can't people understand?

Understanding Jodie
Wasn't hard to do
Understanding all her problems
You haven't got a clue

Oh, to be a Goth
Wearing all the gear
With make up on her face
Why do others fear?

It's me beneath this costume
I am really quite like you
But this is my identity
You could be like me too

Try to get to know me
My desires and my need
All you see is my suffering
And how I seem to bleed

Believe me I am no freak
No rocky horror too
I am not your enemy
No alien to you

PICTURE OF INNOCENCE

She has the face of an angel
With eyes that care
A wonderful girl
With dark flowing hair

Her look of innocence
Right there on her face
Such a nice girl
With elegance and grace

As pure as the driven snow
That settles on the ground
She sends a fine message
With love all around

She appears quite timid
Like a lamb or a deer
But that's part of her appeal
To others so near

She's the type you protect
To keep her from harm
This is why she is popular
She's so full of charm

This was a poem about Kyra featured on the front cover
from an observation of mine as a nurse, from working with
her as a carer.

LIFE (AS WE KNOW IT)
by Stephen Robert Sutton

If you like life then show it
If you like life then let me know it
If you want a rose then
Grow it and show it

Life is just as we know it
Don't look for anything you don't know
Let's live it up
Come on then let's go

Life is just as we know it
With no surprise or mystery
Live your life to the full
Don't you agree?

Don't be afraid to let go
By doing things that you don't know
Like the flower it will help you to grow
And help it along
Do it right and you will never go wrong

The book title explains about life in general and the way most
people feel about it

FEEL GOOD FACTOR
by Stephen Robert Sutton

Do you possess the feel-good factor
This I need to know
Have you got what it takes?
Have you got the get up and go?

Are health and full of strength?
Enough to combat the world around
Or do you just give in
For this is what I have found

Try stretching and building your body
And focus on your mind
Then you gain the inner strength
You thought you had left behind

Eat healthy eat good and its understood
That's all you need for fuel
Plus, a dose of confidence
Make it a useful tool

This is about feeling good about you and about life

MIXED EMOTIONS
by Stephen Robert Sutton

One moment I am happy
One moment I am sad
I reflect on the life I had
It somehow makes me glad

I concentrate on those happy times
To get me through the day
And hope to get some more of them
For this hope and pray

I reflect on my childhood
Memories of yesterday
When I was playing on the swing
I was happy I must say

I played with plastic soldiers
And cars of every kind
Sadly, I grew up
And left my past behind

I deal with mixed emotions
So cheerful and so sad
I still reflect on happy time
And all the fun I had

I started my own family

And the joy was there again
Celebrating all event
I was so happy I can't explain

But life it goes on changing
And I feel this in my heart
My mixed emotion stays with me
They never will depart

So, I learn how to live with it
Controlling all my thoughts
And pull myself together
When I feel out of sorts

SOLITUDE
by Stephen Robert Sutton

I live my life in solitude

It has become the only way to live

The world has been so cruel to me

There are those I can't forgive

My tortured soul lives on

My body is full of pain

I can't maintain my happy thoughts

They are as common as the rain

My spirit has been dampened

My criticism and hate

I need a life line from my life

Before it is too late

Here within my solitude

I reflect now on a thought

A single hope to rescue me

With hope and wisdom brought

Salvation serves as my friend

It's the only one I have now

By taking all my pain away

By death I take a bow

I leave this life so empty

With nothing else to give

They have taken everything from me

Now I don't know how to live

MY SAFE PLACE

by Stephen Robert Sutton

I shelter away
From the monsters' claws
Safely hiding
Within four walls

That creature that menaced me
as a child
Tortured my mind
And drove me wild

Its savage claws
Scratched my skin
And made me bleed
Afraid within

He raped my body
And raped my mind
Killed my soul
And my spirit combined

And now I conceal my safe
In a safe place
But the memories haunt me
I can still see his face

The ugliest man
You could ever find
Is now old and grey
And he is going blind

But still, he scares me
With his menacing voice
So, I killed the monster
I had no choice

Now I spend my life
Within a cell
For he is no longer here
He was sent to hell

I still have nightmares
I see his face
Even though I live in
My safe place

STRENGTH OF MIND AND BODY

by Stephen Robert Sutton

The advice I would like to give to you

Is so profound it must be true

Not to be lazy or shoddy

But strong in mind and body

Exercise for you each day

And keep all that weight at bay

Eat a good diet of vegetables and fruit

And give the old fat a boot

Drink plenty of water flush them kidneys out

Take this good advice and be healthy have no doubt

Eat your fresh cooked fish and your omega 3

Then you can study all your books just you wait and see

Keep your mind healthy

Read and write each day

By doing a quiz or crossword

Your mental ability will stay

You're just as sharp as yesterday

Believe it as a fact

Strength in mind and body

Healthy to be exact

SOFA SURFIN

by Stephen Robert Sutton

I am here looking for a bed
Seeking somewhere to rest my head
Waking up in a strange room
Feeling down and full of gloom

Reflecting on a happier time
Listening to the hours chime
From a clock hanging on the wall
Disillusioned and feeling small

I have to shake this feeling being so blue
People say it's really up to you
This world is what you make it
You must be positive, don't fake it

Sofa surfin is just temporarily
You can be what you want to be
Try to think positively
Being happy and being free

It's a well-known fact
Set yourself a task
Follow your heart desire
Set negativity on fire

This is definitely no bull

Live your life to the full

Don't take from life just give

Now get off that sofa and live

BAGGAGE

by Stephen Robert Sutton

You build your life
On a foundation of truth
And start to develop them
In your youth

Life long journey provides
All you don't need
But life experience can also
Help you succeed

Marriage and children
Are gathered on the way
And can be left behind
That's what I say

Broken relationships
Are like abandon dreams
Like hopes
Ambitions and schemes

Like baggage
It's left at the door
Like the life
You had before

Don't dwell on yesterday

On what could have been

But look to the future

On what you have never seen

MY PET DOG

by Stephen Robert Sutton

I had her from a puppy
Smothered her with love
She is my little treasure
As gentle as a dove

She is a family member
Just like my little cat
Curled up and so cosy
Sleeping on the mat

She grew up so quickly
Not a puppy any more
She loves playing with her toys
Rolling on the floor

My dog is so special
Although she gets in strife
I would never part with her
She's part of life

NOBODY LISTENS

by Stephen Robert Sutton

Nobody listens
Nobody cares
Nobody wants to
Nobody dares

Frightened to speak
Left on the shelf
No one understands
My mental health

Vicious and spiteful
Echoes remain
No one is listening
To those insane

I speak of my illness
My problems in life
You cannot see madness
Not without strife

The darkness is present
The demons appear
You cannot see them
But believe me they're here

Nobody listens
To the words that I say
They think I am sane
But I muddle through the day

One day they will listen
And remember my name
Find my poor body
And say what a shame

Nobody listens
Nobody cares
Nobody wants to
Nobody dares

This poem is about mental illness and how professionals fail
to listen to patients

WHEN I FALL
by Stephen Robert Sutton

Who is going to catch me?

When I fall

Who is going to comfort me?

When I feel small

Are you going to find me?

When I am lost

Will you reimburse me?

For any cost

Are you going to forgive me?

When I do wrong

Are you going to sing me?

A comforting song

When I fall

Will you pick me up

Holding your hands

Like a plastic cup

Will you catch me?

When I fall

Will you make me feel

Ten feet tall

Will you pick me up

When I fall

Comfort me

When I feel small

Written about my childhood seeking help shouting into the wilderness, I hear my voice now and want to rescue myself from the past.

THE GHOST

by Stephen Robert Sutton

I speak to you
About the ghost
To explain it all
It's about a host

A man that carries
A deadly thing
A nasty virus
Or plague like thing

He makes his journey
Far and wide
With this deadly virus
Deep inside

He touches those
Who stands so close
This evil man
Who is called the ghost?

People die
A painful death
With burns and boils
And lack of breath

No one see him

Travelling near and far

But just leave them

With his deadly scar

The ghost could be

Standing by your side

You cannot escape him

You cannot hide

Taken from my story called 'The ghost' about a virus
deadlier than covid 19

SILENT WORLD

by Stephen Robert Sutton

No one knows
The way I feel
But in my world
You know its real

The silent world
I live my days
Without a sound
These are my ways

To see mouths move
Without a sound
Cars and buses
Moving all around

The birds are singing
Dogs bark out loud
Living in my silent world
Is really profound

I miss such a lot
Not hearing at all
I can't hear the clock
Ticking on the wall

We take for granted

What we hear and see

But just for a time

Please think of me

PROFOUND
by Stephen Robert Sutton

Deeply my thoughts are
A philosopher you see
Coping with life
With my degree

With my conviction
My obsession to study
I take my time
I am never in a hurry

My analysis is detailed
Examine the truth
A time for tutorial
While I am in my youth

By my motivation
Self evident I found
Constantly striving
Completely profound

Profound is my name
Because of my thinking you see
Striving to improve
A scholar I shall be

DO YOU SEE ME

by Stephen Robert Sutton

Do you see me?
Do you care?
Am I invisible?
Just in the air

Do you see through me?
Like a ghost in the night
So, do I scare you?
Fill you with fright

You walk right past me
Like I am not there
With no acknowledgement
Like you don't even care

You see only my fault
Like a lantern alight
Showing my madness
The goods not in sight

I look in a mirror
And I see my reflection
Is it really me?
Or just a deception

I want to scream
Just to be seen
Or trash everywhere
Just to be seen

Do you see me?
Could you just care?
Just speak to me
Make me aware

Another example of the feelings of a mental health patient
being ignored by professional people who are supposed to
care

BUILDING YOUR LIFE WITH A SOLID FOUNDATION

by Stephen Robert Sutton

You are building your life
With a solid foundation
Living your life
Without complication

Building your life
With a foundation of love
This is built
By your parent with love

They supply you with
Religion and truth
Starting you off
When you're in your youth

Their political view
Reflecting on you
All their morals
Will follow you too

When you grow up
You choose your own way
And in your life
You hear what they say

Often, we learn from
Our mistakes everyday
But we get through our life
In our own special way

COURAGE

by Stephen Robert Sutton

I live my life

Without any shame

I lived my life

And played the game

I loved and laughed

My whole life through

And kept my cool

With so much to do

I was brave

In a times of concern

In living my life

With lessons to learn

My courage is there

For all to see

Through life's great battles

I came to be

Courage is shared

By a woman or a man

Whoever is like this?

I am their fan

Be it a man or woman

Their story is told

All of their life

Begins to unfold

BELIEVE ME

by Stephen Robert Sutton

What do you believe?

Does it feel real?

Is it a god?

How does it feel?

When do you worship

When do you pray?

Is it in the morning?

At the end of the day

What do you call him?

Has he a name

Is he glorified?

Due to his fame

Is he a messiah?

A guru or king

A Buddha or Mohammed

Or any old thing

Is he so powerful?

Surrounded by fire

Is he supreme

And one you admire

My look at various religions and beliefs of today, where I ask myself why are there so many religions and what makes people follow such teachings.

CRIPPLED WORLD

by Stephen Robert Sutton

Look at the wars

The famine and disease

Are you ashamed?

Are you displeased?

Global warming

Out of control

A crippled world

The world as a whole

Fear of the madness

Living in shame

Is this world a joke

Are we playing a game

Riots and looting

Pointless pursuits

While politicians

Dress up in their suits

Blinded by opinion

Racism and greed

If you cut yourself

Don't you just bleed?

One mucked up world
Crippled within
Isn't it dreadful?
A global sin

So, work together
Don't dither or roam
Repair all the cracks
Make it your home

INJUSTICE

by Stephen Robert Sutton

What you see is in your head

The person you see alas is dead

You think what you do is right

But all it is, is a racist fight

Don't you see we have a right to live?

And it shows by the love we give

we pray to the same god above

And all we want is love

What we see is injustice I say

when all we want to do is pray

Pray for the weak and feeble in mind

I beg you don't be cruel but be kind

Don't judge a man by his skin

but look at the man within

He bleeds red blood like you and I

so don't make his family cry

At the injustice that you create

or you surely deserve the same fate

one bad deed to end the day

by your reckless act, by your display

SO PROFOUND
by Stephen Robert Sutton

My life is complex I have often found
It's twists and turns and is so profound
It is a marvel to me that I am still here
Living my life without any fear

I take all the risks in life you see
And pattern my life like an old tapestry
Working out ways to get through the day
And say all the things that I want to say

I intensely think out my hourly chores
I know what is mine and I know which is yours
I keep all my possessions close to my chest
And choose who I want for a guest

I have flown so high into the clouds
Amidst the silence over the crowds
 Now I keep my feet close to the ground
And think of something so profound

A loose philosophic look at life with a profound look at logic

TRANSITION (The link)

by Stephen Robert Sutton

The link is between life and death
The moment you take your last breath
The transition of life existence
To the point of no resistance

The euphoria of a life beyond life
This place where you know you will strife
To the heavens that you may dream of
Far beyond the stars up above

Where angels glow an eternal light
And drift around in a heavenly flight
With the sound of a heavenly choir
This is where your spirit will retire

A journey from your own living soul
At last, at peace, destiny is your goal
Far is the journey, but by the blink of an eye
You fade out and travel up past the sky

ME AND MY SELVES

by Stephen Robert Sutton

How do I start to explain?

About my life when I was sane

Was it real or was it not

To be honest I have almost forgot

About the trauma and the pain

And about the day I went insane

The brutal things that happened to me

I was once in captivity then set free

My mind was whole and now it's apart

Like the chambers of my heart

First, I am Frank, and then I am John

How I wish I was only one

So many people in one head

Am I Alan or am I now Fred

One moment a boy then I am a man

Trying to reason as much as I can

My mind is so split I can't see the truth

Why was I abused in my youth?

These people protect me those in my head

The only time I am free is when I am in bed

Sleeping so soundly away from all fear
Till someone disturbs me coming so near
Me and my selves conflicting in thought
Tussling in my brain that life is so short

In the evening the child comes along
To tell me a story or sing me a song
And then in came Frank to protect me from harm
Or Fred to keep me quite calm

My personalities are so different you see
But at time I wish they would let me be
It's confusing because why I must share?
All these people, oh what do I care?

PORTRAIT OF MY SOUL

by Stephen Robert Sutton

Paint a picture
On canvas for me
Using colours
That plainly I see

Dark colours of
Purple and grey
Depicting my mood
At the end of the day

Paint it in detail
Like a good photograph
Don't make it funny
Don't make me laugh

Make it so dull
But clear enough to see
Paint me a portrait
Do this for me

You are painting my soul
This looks very real
Paint me a conscience
So, I can feel

Deep in my thoughts
I remember my pain
Scrub it all out
And start it again

THE DARKEST OF DAYS
by Stephen Robert Sutton

I worship my love
And her wildest of ways
To lose her you see
Would be the darkest of days

She determines my thoughts
And rules my life
But never the less
She is my wife

Whatever she does
However, she feels
Her every action
Always appeals

When I lost my heart
To that woman you see
I let it be known
I was as happy as can be

And now at her grave
I think of her ways
This is the worst time
The darkest of days

LIVING WITH A PHOBIA

by Stephen Robert Sutton

Rational fear is natural to us all
Like being on cliff top fearing to fall
Or falling in water thinking you would drown
Or on a ridge fright to jump down

But being frightened of a clown
Watching a show
Your friends want to see it
 But you just want to go

Frightened of a spider or a mouse
Or of noises in your house
What is this irrational fear?
What is this coming near

But phobias are real to you
Who can explain what to do?
Coping with your own mind
With no explanation to find

JOURNEY THROUGH THE MIND OF A KILLER

by Stephen Robert Sutton

Take a journey with me inside the mind
You will never know what you may find
With narrow corridors full of light
Like lots of bulbs oh so bright

Here the deepest thoughts can be found
With such confusion the journey's profound
For here lies, the deepest secrets known to man
So, try to solve it if you can

How the man first fell ill
Or why the man wanted to kill
Was he mad or was he bad
The story really is very sad

As his thought begin to unwind
We see what's in the real mind
In a dark room for hours, he spent
Planning the evil of his own intent

With a murderous intention on his mind
With such brutality is what you will find
That journey you took inside his head
You were the victim and now you're dead

BEING DIFFERENT
by Stephen Robert Sutton

Walking and talking in your own style
Just being you and wearing a smile
Wearing the clothes that you want to wear
Living your life without a care

Just being different showing your worth
The only one of your kind walking this earth
Alone or with company you're not really fussed
Doing what you want that is a must

Just being different to those you're around
Just being there without making a sound
People love you or hate or find you strange
Or they accept you for you'll never change

PROGRESS OF A FOOL
by Stephen Robert Sutton

From a bastard child you begin to grow

Learned all the things you needed to know

About how to steal a loaf of bread

And forget all the things your mother had said

You knew how to hate, you knew how to lie

Take the path of fate and know how to die

Death and destruction you brought on yourself

By treading on others to gain your own wealth

So, die like a fool, for here is your end

You will die alone and without a friend

Even yourself you begin to hate

Showing your feeling now it's too late

Your dying hour, others will never forget

They were right, they won they're bet

They said you would regret the things you have done

And as you die a new life begun

For as one life ends another will start

Let's hope they are better with warmth in their heart.

DEVOTION

by Stephen Robert Sutton

I sacrifice my life for you
I promise to be humble and true
All else I will set apart
And to you I give you my heart

With charity of mind, I devote myself to you
Please observe I am humble and true
You and I will surely understand
That is why I ask for you hand

That we may be one from this day
And let everyone witness what we say
Our vows to be humble and true
You will love only me and I will love only you

And by our devotion we will strive to be
In perfect loving harmony
For richer for poorer better or worse
Join hands and hope that our love lasts the course
No one will divide us our strength shall remain
Listen to my word as I speak so plain

DEPRESSION

by Stephen Robert Sutton

In a dark place far from what I know
In a place so dismal where most fear to go
I linger alone far from my thoughts
Like a leper or a skin full of warts

Like a body disfigured by societies cruel tricks
I am in a bad way, I 'm in a fix
It's hard to explain my feelings you see
This isn't my way this isn't me
I don't eat in the day or show my face
I walk with my head down all over the place

Time passes by me I know not the hour
I am like a machine that has lost all its power
I go deeper and deeper in a dark pit
I don't care about life I don't give a shit
Without taking these pills I would surely be dead
Please help me escape from what lies ahead

SCARS

by Stephen Robert Sutton

Be who you want to be
Do what you want to do
Live how you want to live
It's up to you

Forget what you need to forget
It's all in the past
Live for the present
It's with you at last

The scars do remind you
Of your past life that has been
Some scars are hidden
They will never be seen

Plan for your future
Trips far ahead
But don't dream about them
You can't reach them from your bed

PARADOX

by Stephen Robert Sutton

You speak to me about many things

About commitments and wedding ring

Good fortune and things so profound

I hear you and the way you sound

But its self contradiction and false proposition

A life time of such hope and such superstition

The inconsistency is blowing my mind

By making me confused and totally blind

This paradoxical life that I lead

Makes life a lie and a dependable need

Full of senselessness and absurdity

It's no kind of life it means nothing to me

It is no answer it is catch twenty-two

It's nothing like me or nothing like you

It's an enigma or ambiguity

It certainly means nothing to me

A mystery or an oddity

Is this the way I should be

It is full of inconsistency

A simple life or a prelude to me

THE SHROUDED FIGURE

by Stephen Robert Sutton

The darkness came so suddenly
And coldness filled the air
The corridors were dimly lit
And my heart filled with despair

A figure then appeared
As cold as the night
Moving slowly as it did
Give me such a fright

A shrouded figure
Of a monk appeared before my eyes
He was so mysterious
Wearing this disguise

Dark and menacing was his look
Like he just stepped from a grave
A fearless creature he appeared
I was frightened and not so brave

Written after working in a monastery or priory, very spooky
place where the shrouded monk has been seen

DROWNING

by Stephen Robert Sutton

I had a dream
About how life could be
I was alone
And I was floating in the sea

I was clinging hold of
Some sort of raft
It was a man made
Floating craft

Suddenly I let go
Of the side
And drifted with
The flowing of the tide

I panicked as my body
Drifted down
Because I knew
That I would certainly drown

I was ashamed
About the way I had behaved
As a ship arrived
And I was saved

The moral of the story

Is to never give in

Be positive in life

And you will win

ABANDONMENT

by Stephen Robert Sutton

Left alone in the middle of a town

Standing alone in a lonely place

In the midst of chaos

With worry on your face

This is abandonment

Left in a desert without water

Walking in the heat of the sun

Thirsty and starving feeling faint

And this condition has only just begun

This is abandonment

You were

Left in a jungle in the wild

Feeling so lost and helpless

As a young child

This is abandonment

Your frustration

With no education

The world seems dark

It never seems bright

You live in darkness
Never seeing light

Abandoned and lost
Without any hope
How do you see life?
When you're unable to cope

This is abandonment

THE TRAVELLER
by Stephen Robert Sutton

Wherever I roam
I love to return home
To a familiar place
And part of my race

I travel so far
To a distant land
With many mountains
Or lots of sand

To Japan or Thailand
I travel so far
I journeyed by sea
To the USSR

Across to America
All over the USA
And over to Canada
For a long stay

I dream of my journeys
The trips that I make
To far away countries
New ventures I take

Over to Sweden where my friend lives

It is the second home for me
So many places to go to
Lots of scenery to see

I take lots of pictures
From journeys untold
Something to look back on
For when I grow old

THE PERSON WITHIN

by Stephen Robert Sutton

Can you see me?
I am here
Are you looking at me?
It isn't clear

I can hear you
And I can see
It's so frustrating
What has happened to me?

I cannot speak
But I am aware
I can feel a breeze
In the air

My crippled body
Is here with me
My eyes are blurry
But I can see

Is this the life?
That I must live
Confined to a bed
With nothing to give

Being fed through a tube
It's not for me
I don't approve
It's a liberty

The nurse comes
To wash me down
They smile at me
Sometimes they frown

They drain the urine
From my urine bag
As I lie here
It's such a drag

Some play music
They laugh and sing
And cheer me up
All that sort of thing

If only they knew
How I really felt inside
Do they care?
That I just want to hide

I do appreciate
What they do
But look at me

This could be you

So please be patient
Have empathy
Remember the person
I used to be

GATHERING DUST

by Stephen Robert Sutton

Visiting houses
Smelling all the items full of must
Everything around me is
Gathering dust

Dirty curtains hanging down
Full of dust all around
Things that make you
Choke and sneeze
Like the finest flowers
In a breeze

That blows the pollen
In the air
Seeing all this I despair

Like life has faded
Or stood still
It makes me sick
It makes me ill

It's such a shame
The state of this place
It's in a mess
Everything is out of place

It reminds me of life
When times at an end
Nobody knows exactly
What's round the bend?

THE ONLY WAY TO LIVE

by Stephen Robert Sutton

Don't live your life
Thinking about negative things
For with every death
A new life begins

It's part of nature
Just one of those things
Death takes a life
And a new life begins

Live your life positively
While you are in your youth
Be a good person
And always tell the truth

Obey the laws of the land
Live life in peace
Be a good person
Let hate decrease

Smile even if
You are in pain
Think of those
Bad or insane

Those that need help
To get by in life
Don't let them suffer
Or live in strife

Better yourself
And others you trust
Live for the present
This is a must

FADED PICTURE

by Stephen Robert Sutton

Walking through a gallery
Admiring the art
Many fine painting
Where an earth can I start

I found a faded picture
Hanging on the wall
It was a portrait of a woman
Standing proud and tall

The faded picture
Showed her image so fair
This beautiful lady
With long flowing hair

With her hazel eyes
And green satin long dress
She was like an angel

She looked very kind
With a radiant smile
She dressed so elegantly
With such a nice style

She came from the past

A by gone age
She held herbs in her hand
That was probably sage

I sat for a while
Imagining this time past
With warmth in my heart
The time past so fast

She must spend ages
Sitting for the pose
I was here for a long time
Until the gallery closed

The image of the picture
Stayed clear in my head
That faded picture
Remained until I went to bed

I fell asleep
And to my surprise
I dreamt about her
With those large hazel eyes

THE GHOST Part Two
by Stephen Robert Sutton

The ghost continues with his mighty dread

For his enemies he puts them to their bed

With his deadly virus he claims your life

Spares no mercy with his deadly strife

With his bitter heart and callous mind

He has no feelings, he is not kind

His virus spreads from soul to soul

He knows his objective or his final goal

He reaps destruction wherever he goes

And where he is no one knows

He cannot be seen beneath his invisible shroud

He walks about within a cloud

He seeks to find his victims near

His evil intentions are very clear

To clear the earth of human kind

Without a trace and nothing to find

FEEL GOOD FACTOR

by Stephen Robert Sutton

Do you possess the feel-good factor

This I need to know

Have you got what it takes?

Have you got the get up and go?

Are health and full of strength?

Enough to combat the world around

Or do you just give in

For this is what I have found

Try stretching and building your body

And focus on your mind

Then you gain the inner strength

You thought you had left behind

Eat healthy eat good and its understood

That's all you need for fuel

Plus, a dose of confidence

Make it a useful tool

MY LOVE OF SWEDEN

by Stephen Robert Sutton

Wherever I travel
Wherever I roam
Sweden is
My second home

With its wonderful landscape
Forests and deer
I long to visit
With friends that are dear

I have been there each season
Spring, summer autumn and winter too
My heart is right there
With all of you

My many friends
Greet me with love and cheer
I can't wait to go there
And have them so near

My first visit to Sweden
Just captured my heart
Ever since then
I found it difficult to depart

Some of my greatest moment
I share with them all
I now cherish such memories
That I can recall

I visit Sweden
Whenever I can
I love Sweden
I am the countries best fan

SPIRAL
by Stephen Robert Sutton

I feel my body
Spiralling down
Lower and lower
Right down to the ground

Spinning so fast
Out of control
Out of a cloud
And into a hole

Going right down
With a shudder and twist
And finally arriving
Into an abyss

With a fire around me
I could certainly tell
I wasn't in heaven
I was in hell

Secured in chains
Bound so tightly
With no one to rescue me
Or set me free

When I awoke

0From this awful nightmare

My body was bruised

But I didn't care

The chain that was binding

My legs and my wrist

You didn't expect that

This rhyme is a twist

AWAKEN

by Stephen Robert Sutton

Awake from your slumber

And join reality

There is a world out there

Waiting for thee

You're so blind

So, negative you cannot see

Take stock of reality

Set the world free

There is poverty

Starvation and malnutrition and all

Battles and a risk

Of a nuclear war

People go to sleep

Full of despair

Theres fog on the streets

Are you aware?

So, awake to the world

That you claim to love

Such cloudy skies

Just look above

Wake up to the world
Before it's too late
Wake up, wake up
Or live with this fate

DIFFERENT AGAIN

by Stephen Robert Sutton

I am an individual
One of a kind
Just different
That's all you will find

I am my person
With my own kind of style
With a winning personality
And a happy smile

I live my life
In my own special way
Just living
For each and every day

I really don't care
What people may think
I have fun in life
And know how to drink

I am so in control
And know what I need
And when I get cut
I know how to bleed

I care about myself
And all my basic needs
And like other dyslexic people
Whose life succeeds

I don't need riches
Nor fame, I can be poor
As long as I get no abuse
From people anymore

I have my opinion
Talents to show
And if you mock me
I will tell you where to go

LIFE'S JOURNEY

by Stephen Robert Sutton

Throughout life there is a journey
With pit stops on the way
Changing periods of your life
Learning every day

Learning from experience
Reaching every goal
Working hard to feed your kin
Then you rest your weary soul

You live your childhood
Going to a school
You sing and play
Acting like a fool

Your teenage years are sometimes wasted
Rebelling against your peers
Protesting and moaning
You live out all your fears

Your working life
Is such a chore
Working for pittance
Makes you poor

You finally retire
Towards journeys end
You can't do what you want
And so, you pretend

Finally, life's journey ends
And you have done your best
You have done all you can
So, leave it to the rest

JOURNEY WITH ME

by Stephen Robert Sutton

Come on a journey with me
Through the galaxies
To another planet
Or just to ecstasy

Travel through the clouds
Flying like birds everywhere
Without any concerns
And without a care

Drifting over field
And valleys far below
I can show you any place
If you want to go

Journey with me
Travel with my very soul
Forget all you're past
Abandon your goal

Just with me
On earth or in space
It's simply your choice
About the journey you face

I will help you with your future

Your plans and your schemes

Please journey with me

And I will forfill all your dreams

THE MEDITATION GARDEN

by Stephen Robert Sutton

Relax in your garden

Like you're in a dream

Like floating on clouds

Or travelling down stream

Let your mind drift

Right up to the shore

Like on a grass bank

The do it some more

Surrender your thoughts

And pressures of life

Don't think past worries

Bad feelings or strife

Just be at peace

Let yourself go

Take all your anxieties

And just let them go

My meditation gardens

Is a place I can rest

Filled with my plants

With this I am blessed

Filled with my comforts
In my garden living free
Part of my own world
A life in tranquillity

THE AUTHOR'S TRUE IDENTITY

by Stephen Robert Sutton

The author works relentlessly
For hours and hours each day
Spending hours typing down
Producing what he will say

Carefully thinking out his plot
His characters seem near
Each living in his head
Gradually they do appear

With spoken words of wisdom
Often said in jest
They come alive within the page
Each he knows is best

He studies every person
That seems to come his way
And just imagine his characters
And all the things they'd say

The writer studies such people
In his or her own way
And so, the story is written
By the end of day

The author could be any sex
And this is often clear
By the way they write they're lines
And make their sex quite clear

The style, the characters tell you so
Although they change their name
Man or woman you can tell
They are often never the same

The author's true identity
Are found within the pages of the book
By reading the style of the story
So please take a look

SUNDAY

by Stephen Robert Sutton

You settle down at night
Counting all those sheep
Till the cock crows in the morning
And wakes you from your sleep

The cows are passing by your window
Heading for the farm
Trekking from a quiet pathway
They will do no harm

The church bells are ringing
As loud as can be
People dressed in Sunday clothes
For everyone to see

There are lots of children playing out
At the start of day
With neighbours talking over the fence
With so much to say

Men are walking down the street
Heading to the pub
While other people go to church
And worship god above

Sunday dinner is on the table
So that we can eat
Come together as a family
With everyone to greet

Finally, we rest at night
Watching our TV
Many programs that we like
A lot for us to see

Teatime comes in the evening
With sandwiches and cake
Sometimes we eat trifle
For our stomachs sake

We prepare ourselves for the night
Prepare our night attire
With our hot coco in our hands
Snuggled by the fire

THESE OLD BOOTS

by Stephen Robert Sutton

I was looking through my cupboard
To see what I could find
I came across some old battered boots
I am sure you know the kind

Scuffed and battered leather boots
I use to wear everyday
Just left in this cupboard
Just to fade away

The souls were cracked
And the heels wear worn down
The tops were flattened
And no laces I had found

I tried them on just to see
If they fitted any more
I must admit I found they did
And my wife threw them out the door

They are old and so tatty
You can't wear them again
I said yes, I can
When I am gardening in the rain

I found I could not part with them

They were part of my life

And if it came to it

I would sooner ditch my wife

ALI'S VINDALOO

by Stephen Robert Sutton

Ali made a curry
It was said to be so hot
He found the hottest spices
And put them in the pot

He mixed it all with herbs
Mix vegs and the lot
Mixed it all together
In Ali's super pot

He tested his new curry
And felt that it was fine
He got his ingredient from a store
In Ashton under Lyne

Vindaloo he called it
But they called it windy loo
The victims that ate it
Had a proper to do
Victims sitting on the loo
Feeling in a stew

As hot as it went in
It burned when it came out
They should sue That Ali

With this have no doubt

I do curse Ali
For my hot steamy poo
And my hot ring
From his god dam hot Vindaloo

THE NARCISSIST

by Stephen Robert Sutton

He controls the moves you make
With the seed that he has sown
He takes away you very will
And leaves totally alone

Your life is not yours to live
But to forgiveness you do think
His evil traits that he dreams
He thrives on each of your screams

His jealousy encourages his rage
The money he takes from your wage
He controls your money
And your wealth
He affects your general health

Mental and physical abuse
Gives him power and control so profuse
Leaving you without a relative or friend
Beware he will kill you in the end

SOMEONE WHO CARES

by Stephen Robert Sutton

She is the person that you contact
In times of desperate need
She helps you at work
So that you may succeed

She's sensitive to others needs
She has a glowing charm
Takes new staff under her wing
Protects them from harm

The other care staff loves you
You're their starring light
By the way you shine in everyone's eyes
You stand out so bright

You use your skills to your best
With confidence and pride
Although you are nervous
And sensitive deep inside

You are someone who is loyal
Part of a winning team who shares
By treating everyone as equal
You are someone who cares

TO THOSE WHO CARE

by Stephen Robert Sutton

To those who care so relentlessly
Who work through the day and night?
Those who serve the greatest good
And won't give in without a fight

We celebrate your kindness,
Your compassion everyday
Your tireless efforts to help everyone
And for your good health we pray

The gallant and the eager
Who feel they are forgotten
You work and just expect some thank
And not be treated rotten

To be remembered for what you do
It a bonus in itself
With happy smiles upon your face
And not left upon a shelf

Good humour is a plus
It gets you through the day
And the odd thanks from management
That's all I can say

MY SAFE PLACE (Part Two)

by Stephen Robert Sutton

I feel at ease in a cupboard or wardrobe
Hiding away from harm
Like a safe room built especially for me
With my own burglar alarm

I try to think of happy times
When my child existed of innocents within
When no one abused me
And I had never heard of sin

I reflect on happy times
Like my trips to the sea
Or days in the park
When my life was free

I often think of good times
I remember them so well
It makes me feel so special
While I am living in this hell

I cut myself to get relief
No one will understand
I just want security
Like holding someone's hand

I get relief from the flowing blood
Although I know it's wrong
I tell you this in my memory
For this is my swan song

I never meant to kill myself
I think I cut too deep
But rest assured I am safe from harm
I am permanently asleep

MISTAKEN IDENTITY

by Stephen Robert Sutton

I walked through a misty field
In a wood very near
A body was found dead
How it happened was unclear

The police were searching both far and wide
For a knife, as he had been stabbed in his side
As investigation did proceed and evidence was sort
A man confessed to the crime because he was caught

He was questioned about the crime
As his DNA was found at the time
He admitted that he stabbed with a knife
And ended this poor man's life

But it was a mistake
It wasn't meant to be
It was the wrong man
A case of mistaken identity

He was ashamed as he bowed his head
He was so upset the wrong man was dead
He had stabbed the man again and again
He acted like a man insane

The man he wanted had killed his wife
The same as he did with a knife
He enraged seeing her body so
Covered in blood, he was full of woe

He persuades the person
He thought it would be
Into the mist
Where he hardly could see

He discovered when he turned the body round
That it wasn't the man lying on the ground
When he discovered what he had found out
He confessed his crime which left them no doubt

He was guilty of the crime in hand
And charged him with the crime
A mistaken identity
And for that he is doing time

SUPER HUMAN

by Stephen Robert Sutton

With the strength of a gorilla

Or a mighty bear

He tosses a large vehicle

Right up in the air

He can make holes in walls and

Kick down a door

And does it with ease

Like large charging boar

Another super human

Demonstrates her strength in style

By throwing up many cars

And lands them in single file

Another one just runs

For miles every day

Like a long-distance runner

Running all the way

Super human beings

Have special gifts you see

They can do many things

I wish that they were me

SECRETS

by Stephen Robert Sutton

People hid their secrets
Disguised so non can see
Revealing what they like
Or what they want to be

Some secrets hide their shame
Like a mask for their disguise
They shelter from the truth
Revealing all their lies

But soon they get found out
From the darkness they conceal
The abundance of their sins
Soon becomes very real

THE RAVEN (Part Two)
by Stephen Robert Sutton

Searching for its victim

Day by day

The dark figure of this

Bird of prey

The raven is known

Everywhere to kill

With her screeching sound

Giving you a chill

She is human

Although you would never know

A schizophrenic

Always on the go

She seeks revenge

For the murder of a friend

And is known

To get you in the end

A fearful woman

With madness in her eyes

She is sure to

Take you by surprise

Her large sharp claws
Stab you in the chest
While her speed and strength
Deals with the rest

She is vicious,
Cunning and mad
All that is evil
And definitely bad

Raven is definitely
Not your friend
The raven will
Get you in the end

Taken from a story called 'Cracked Porcelain'

THE ADVENTURES OF THE TIME TRAVELLING WITCHES

Natasha and Crystal began their journey
Seeking out the past
Time travelling across the universe
Isn't it a blast?

Through ages of black magic
Forming a new bond
Travelling through time
With the waving of their wand

Searching through their destiny
Where do they start?
By seeking out their ancestors
Deep within their heart

But darkness seems to follow them
Evil finds it way
Searching through the history book
Researching day by day

They travel through the centuries
Seeking answers everywhere
But what lurk around the corner
Examine it if you dare

CHILDHOOD FRIENDSHIP

by Stephen Robert Sutton

Childhood is precious, memories are their

Playing so nicely without a care

With childhood friendships

Those memories to share

Living your life without danger or despair

Protected by parent or guardian of a kind

Leaving your worries so far behind

The greatest time or years of your life

With no concerns no fear or strife

Playing so innocent with games of all kinds

With new discoveries sharing your finds

We all have someone a childhood friend

Someone special loyal to the end

SOMEWHAT SUBDUED

I confess to myself
The way that I am
Life is intolerable
And such a sham

Existing at home
Hiding from a disease
Afraid of the virus
Frightened to sneeze

I am somewhat subdued
Feeling so strange
Hoping for a cure
And then life can change

Bitterness takes over
This incredible dread
Living an existence
I might as well be dead

But when I see the state
Then others are in
I look forward in hope
With a confident grin

RISK

We risk are life
In so many ways
By being alive in this world
And exist in a haze

The dangers you see
Are futile to some
The battles we have
And some of them won

We think with our head
But sometimes our heart
We consider the risks
Right from the start

We make decisions
Those are not always right
We make mistakes
And then get in a fight

CLOSE TO MY HEART

I have loved you
From the very start
You are part of me
Close to my heart

Your love astounds me
And makes me feel good
I think that I love you
The way that I should

Love has no boundaries
Open and pure
I love you madly
And there is no cure

I know that I love you
And we will never part
You are my loved one
Close to my heart

CREATURE OF HABIT

It should be noted
The way that I am
I am a creature of habit
And don't give a dam

I live my life fully
To my own gratification
Take care of myself
In any situation

Nobody rules me
I do as I please
Nothing will harm me
No stupid disease

I have a routine
That I follow to the letter
But I always strive
To do better and better

COMPLEX NEEDS

Some people have complex needs
This is considered a fact
They may not function the way we do
For their bodies not in tact

They need help in many ways
So, we give a helping hand
By feeding and dressing
And to help them understand

We make a type of care plan
Of all the things they need
Giving details of the help they require
Helping them to succeed

We look at all the areas
Their activities for living
And try to make life simple
With all the care we are giving

We share our knowledge with others
It's the kind of things we do
Then you can help us with the care
It all depends on you

FUNDAMENTALLY SOUND

You are a unique person
This is what I have found
You're really quite a character
Fundamentally sound

I like you for your complexity
When you're with me it's ecstasy
You are the person meant for me
Fundamentally sound

You change just like a chameleon
By the way you are so reasoning
You fade into the background
And observe without a sound

Helping when you need to help
Your manner is exact
You want to be so versatile
This is a well-known fact

You are a unique person
This is what I have found
You're really quite a character
Fundamentally sound

MANCHESTER AND BEYOND

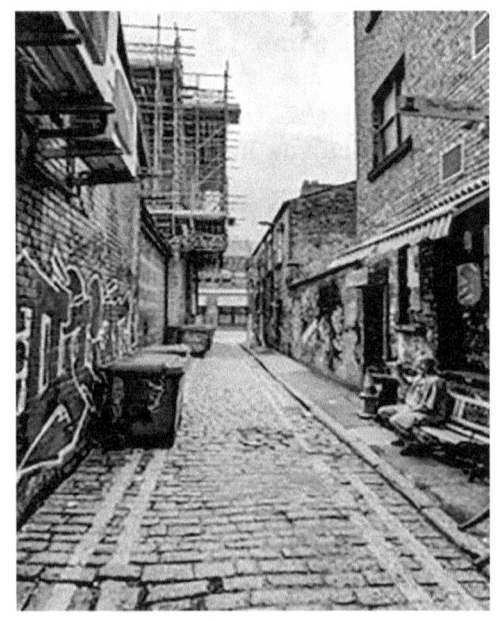

CHILDS PLAY
by Stephen Robert Sutton

Taking all my children
All around the park
Playing on the swings
Singing like a lark

Sitting in the park
Watching everyone
Lying on the grass
Basking in the sun

Splashing in the water
Playing in the sand
Going down the slide
I give a helping hand

Happy children
Shout away
Tired by the
End of day

Night time comes
It's time for bed
Time top rest
Weary head

IN OUR DARKEST DAYS
by Jack Tomlinson

In our darkest of days, Hollow Eyes
What lies beneath these hollow eyes?

We look to the skies.
No elegant beauty,
Nor fading of heart.
In the quietening of spirits, we're drifting apart.

What can we gain,
And what can be lost?
Is there life in these depths
Or the passing across?
Will salvation answer on the uprising sun,
Or will God smile and beckon you, 'Come.'

From the tiniest of seed
To the strongest of flower,
From the crumbling stone wall
To the mightiest tower,
Please don't give in.
Don't give up the fight,
As the morning is calling,
Surviving the night.
The brightest star in heaven is having its say.
Down come Gods angels to take you away.

Alas,

The toughest of decisions

That should never be made,

As they switch off the machine and your eyes start to fade.

Tears will fall,

But memories don't die.

Now, just like the angels,

You'll look down from the sky, But not with hollow eyes,

Nor under these false pretences, nor being enslaved

Inside technology's fences.

Away you'll soar

Through the moonlit bay,

In the valleys of heaven,

No torment to pay.

And there you'll climb the candle lit mast, In elegance and

beauty.

At peace at last

Jack Tomlinson ©

"FOR KING AND COUNTRY"
By Carl Anthony Waldron

My name is private Wilfred Wood

I came from Hazel Grove

I snipered from the trenches

I marched through sand and cove

I fought for King and Country

My rifle it stayed true

My VC cross shines for the men

Who lost their lives for you

We stood upon the battlefields

Each soldier young and brave

We fired into the hillsides

We trudged through muddy grave

We fought for King and Country

In Italy near Rome

Red poppies grow for all the men

Who never made it Home

I came home hailed a hero

To tunes of marching bands

I cried for all my comrades

Who'd died in far off lands

We fought for King and Country

Until your War was won

Red poppies bleed for all the folk

Who lost their soldier son

FREEDOM is a virtue

It can take a Man to War
FREEDOM is a lonely road
That We March on Evermore.

By Carl Anthony Waldron

MANCHESTER TALENT

by Stephen Robert Sutton

As I look around Manchester
What do I find?
So much talent
It blows my mind

Such gifted people
And that's the truth
So much talent
In all our youth

Artist, musicians, writers
So many to find
Some that are homeless
Many you will find

People of all ages
With promising skills
So much creativity
It gives me the chills

Look at this city
See what you have got
Many fine crafts
They have the lot

Manchester's heritage
The talents are rich
Look at their work
And what they accomplish

So just recognise them
Just take a glance
Let them show you their talent
Please give them a chance

MANCHESTER PRISON (STRANGE WAYS)

by Stephen Robert Sutton

How odd me thinks
The strange bleak place
Where thieves and rogues do go
To think of things of yesterday
Or strange ways if you must know

Manchester prison was once known
By its in mates and officers too
Strange ways were just the place
Where prisoners were welcomed to

A tower stood with a watchful guard
Watching a prisoner escape in plight
They watched him leave and knew for well
The police would catch him later at night

The prison warden paced up and down
Keeping a watchful eye
The prisoners were clear what to do
As they stole the governor's pie

What was best there for the rest
Then fifteen years or a five-year stretch
Doing your porridge fulfilling the time
Doing your penance for doing the crime

THE MANCUNIAN

by Stephen Robert Sutton

The Mancunian stands tall and proud
The Mancunian is very loud
He stands up for what he believes
And is proud of what he achieves

The Mancunian is so very bright
The Mancunian can put up a fight
He defends those all around
A Mancunian stands his ground

A Mancunian is proud to be
Part of his society
Standing tall standing lean
Support his football team

The Mancunian may be rich or maybe poor
He may appear at your front door
Laughing and joking with all around
It's not unusual just profound

The Mancunian remains tall and proud
He also remains very loud
He is outspoken just like the rest
But he remains one of the best

Carl Anthony Waldron

I wrote a poem in honour of Our great City and Our beautiful Bees.

"Manchester Oh Manchester"

It doesn't really matter
If you're a red or blue
And we don't give a dam
If your rains soak us through
We love our northern city
Where everyone stands tall
We love our northern city
We're united till we fall.
Manchester Oh Manchester
Please play a song for me
You're in my blood
You're in my bones
And set my Spirit free
It doesn't really matter
If you're a black or white
And we don't give a dam
If you're a wrong or right
We love our northern city
Through its good times and pain
We love our northern city
Through its sunshine and its rain.
It doesn't really matter
On religion or your faith
And we don't give a dam
If you're a beggar or a waif
We love our northern city

And our battles will be won

We love our northern city

And our Bees that make us one.

Manchester Oh Manchester

Please play a song for me

You're in my blood

You're in my bones

And set my Spirit free

Manchester Oh Manchester

Please play a song for me

You're in my blood

You're in my bones

And set my Spirit free.

God Bless all our Mancy Bees this Christmas time.

May they all rest in peace xxx

And God bless Carl Anthony Waldron for his poems and song which will be remembered, following his untimely death in 2020. One of his songs were performed by Ashton Lane called Barefoot Madonna about Joan Baez

ONE LOVE MANCHESTER

by Stephen Robert Sutton

If ever I was emotional
It was seeing a concert occur
I watched the performers
And suddenly my eyes would blur

Top performers sang their tune
Giving freely of their time
For those who died so senselessly
Isn't it such a crime?

Some where over the rainbow
Was Ariana Grande's song
She sang it so beautifully
With not a single note wrong

People hugged all over town
So many people cried
Flowers lay in the street
For all who had died

One love concert for Manchester
And the cities great despair
What an incredible atmosphere
Love was in the air

So, remember one love Manchester

Keep it in your heart

For this city came together

And will never part

Following the horrific time of the terrorist attack in
Manchester arena MEN 22nd May 2017 at the Ariana Grande
concert, a concert was held on 4th June 2017 in memory
of those who died called the 'one love concert' Ariana
Grande returned to host this with many celebrity guests in
Manchester cricket ground.

UNITED IN GRIEF

by Stephen Robert Sutton

I remember thee
At the sadness of the day
I stand and pray
Where the flower lay

Where people come
Across the street not murmuring a sound
The quietness showing respect
Tragedy they found

The senseless murder of local folk
It's such a senseless crime
Blown away and left for dead
Cut off in their prime

But all of you from Manchester
Witness an event so brief
Mourning side by side
United in your grief

People come and help them
Helping those in need
By giving of themselves
With courage they succeed

A concert is arranged

Raising money to help the cause

Showing solidarity

And a reason to end terrorist wars

MANCHESTER PRIDE

by Stephen Robert Sutton

Experience the rainbow
And support them if you may
No matter what's your sexuality
Being straight or being gay

Join the large procession
Travelling down the street
Transsexuals and all kinds
People you must meet

Manchester pride is happening
All those that count today
Demonstrate their freedom
And their right to be gay

They dress in many colours
Like a rainbow in the sky
Stand and cheer them onward
As they wave and pass you by

Canal Street is alive
It is a bustling place
The queens of Manchester
Never look out of place

So, join the pride of Manchester
With their banners flying high
And the rainbows of this world
Will shine in the sky

BELIEVE ME
by Stephen Robert Sutton

What do you believe?

Does it feel real?

Is it a god?

How does it feel?

When do you worship

When do you pray?

Is it in the morning?

At the end of the day

What do you call him?

Has he a name

Is he glorified?

Due to his fame

Is he a messiah?

A guru or king

A Buddha or Mohammed

Or any old thing

Is he so powerful?

Surrounded by fire

Is he supreme

And one you admire

My look at various religions and beliefs of today, where I ask myself why are there so many religions and what makes people follow such teachings.

CROWDED PLACES

by Stephen Robert Sutton

No spaces on the buses
No room on the trains
Too many people round me
You would think they had no brains

I hate such crowded places
No room to sit or breath
This is why I get so anxious
I really want to leave

I push my way through crowds
And run to a quiet place
To gather up my courage
For the journey I must face

The madness of the people
Rushing through the masses
People caught up by the turn styles
With their railway passes

Going through the markets
Madness everywhere
Pushing through the crowds
People never care

DEMONSTATION

by Stephen Robert Sutton

The crowd all gathered
And marched down the street
With lighted torches
And banners with slogans
Made from a sheet

With penned in frustration
Let out in anger you see
The angry crowd are
Coming towards me

Some breaking away
Burning vehicles, breaking things apart
Looting the shops
And leaving their mark

An innocent girl
Is injured on the way
Making her one of many
By the end of the day

The police form a line
For a defence
Attacked by bottles and missiles
Causing offence

One man is left bleeding
In the street all alone
Lying there dead
Holding his phone

The last text he made
To his wife it said
I love you dear
And then he was dead

A LOVER's QUEST

I have searched horizons far and wide,
And tricked the sands of time,
Sailed seven seas,
And chased four winds,
In hope that She'd be mine.
I have sat upon the moon on high,
And slept on clouds above,
Tiptoed through stars,
Jumped Venus and Mars,
In hope to gain Her love.
I have prayed to God on bended knee,
Soared with Angels in the sky,
Danced with Devil,
And sold my soul,
In hopes to hear Her sigh.
I have climbed all hill and mountainside,
Followed every map and chart,
Crossed desert plains,
And all terrains,
In hope to win Her heart

Have You Ever Written a Poem?
Tony Longfella Walsh is apparently our renowned and ac-
claimed Poet of Manchester.
But there are many other poets out there within our fantabu-
lous City.

Including homeless people and buskers etc etc etc.
I myself am fortunate not to be any of the above, but some
say I can write odes...
Written by Carl Anthony Waldron

REFLECTIONS

by Stephen Robert Sutton

Reflections in the waters
The faces that we see
Made from our own memories
Looking back at me

Reflections in a mirror
An image of my face
With eye that are the mirror of my soul
Peer within my life is whole

Reflections speaks about myself
Like rows of tins upon a shelf
Each tin is part of my mind
With no empty ones you will find

Reflections based upon a time
When mother tells a nursery rhyme
Or father tells a fairytale
Of a dragon with a long sharp tail

Reflecting truth and fantasy
Telling what things used to be
Memories of a past concern
Is one way that we must learn

Reflections of my past looking back at the time of the covid
19 virus 2020

INTO DARKNESS

by Stephen Robert Sutton

Into the darkness I came to be

Into the darkness and looking at me

Seeing the person that I once was

Judging the person as anyone does

Helpless and hopeless I used to be

Acting so blindly unable to see

So weak in my mind and broken apart

I hear the sound of the beat of my heart

Anxious and nervous so much afraid

I wish someone would come to my aid

Help me to release all this pain deep inside

With no where to run to nowhere to hide

Fear is the enemy hope is the key

Chased by my past catching up with me

Into the darkness I hide my own past

Till someone finds me and frees me at last

In the bleakness of depression during the covid 19 corona
virus 2020

MORAL GUIDANCE

by Stephen Robert Sutton

The course is set
For you to go
The destination
Is clear you know

Your parent or peers
Set the trail
For moral guidance
So, don't you fail?

A blue print or map
Is drawn for you
Showing you
Just what to do

Whether it's straight
Or crooked you see
Follow the course
To what must be

Moral guidance
Is set from the start
So, do you follow?
Your head or your heart

So, follow your morals

And just you see

And just act

The best you can be

I LOVE MY WORRIOR

(My daughter is a nurse and I wrote this after covid had arrived 2020)
written by Robin Rich

They're choking on darkness

With no end in sight.

Afraid that they may

Be alone in this fight.

The captain is lying

And weapons are gone.

Yet weary from battle

They still carry on.

We worry and wonder

And ask ourselves why?

Not finding an answer

We look to the sky.

We cry, sometimes scream,

Beat our chest, pull our hair.

Oh God can you hear us?

Oh Lord are you there?

The enemy demands that

Our lives must be changed.

And the world as we know it

Has been rearranged.

Though lost in confusion

They're still standing tall.
A ship without compass
They answer the call.

Though the warriors are
Weary they have to prevail.
They're given no option
to win, lose or fail.

One day the enemy
Will have to retreat,
And having once fallen
We'll rise to our feet.

A new day is coming,
A new story to tell,
Of battle born warriors,
Who served us so well.

Robin Rich 2020

LOCK DOWN

by Stephen Robert Sutton

Here I am in a room

Feeling low full of gloom

This is what I see

The walls are closing in on me

Making use of the day

Families pass the time away

Being many or a few

They all find things to do

Children given little chores

And learn to play indoors

Home work takes part of the day

Baking cake for enjoyment they say

Families will swobble invading their space

All huddled together all in one place

End this covid virus some will pray

While some find activities best suits their day

Written at the start of the covid 19 pandemic 2020

PRAYER FOR RECOVERY

by Stephen Robert Sutton

I pray to God

That I survive

This awful virus

And stay alive

My friends have all been

Laid to rest

And live in heaven

Where they are blessed

Please let me recover

To tell the tale

I will always follow you

And never fail

Written at the time of the covid 19 pandemic

PANDEMIC
by Stephen Robert Sutton

Fear the virus
That comes your way
It's taking weak souls
The helpless this day

Thousands are fighting it
Its world wide you see
It's taken my friends
and its now after me

There is nowhere to run to
Nowhere to hide
It will surely get you
If you are outside

A pandemic attack
On hospital wards
We fight the attacks
By remaining indoors

Doctors and nurses
Are in the front-line defence
Fighting the virus
Its so intense

So go to your homes
Just hide away
Come out when its safe
A much brighter day

Written from my experience of the Covid 19 pandemic of 2020

Wearing masks and two metre distancing and now read the following information

What is the velocity of a sneeze that's what you need to know and understand. Is it two metres or beyond this is vital information if you want to stay safe. Sneezes are speedy. "Sneezes travel at about 100 miles per hour," says Patti Wood, author of Success Signals: Understanding Body Language. She adds that a single sneeze can send 100,000 germs into the air.
A cough can travel as fast as 50 mph and expel almost 3,000 droplets in just one go. Sneezes win though—they can travel up to 100 mph and create upwards of 100,000 droplets.9 Apr 2020

LIVING A COMPLEX LIFE

by Stephen Robert Sutton

Living life in complexity
That's what my life seems to be
With winding roads and a busy street
Nothing is straight, regimented or neat

With every day a complication
Try living life with such frustration
Roaming through life with no obligation
So much to do in my situation
Why can't I live with simplification?
Instead of a life of condemnation

Why my life can't be simplified
I want to run away, I want to hide
I sit with a blanket wrapped up inside
Shivering and rocking like my brain has died

And those dreaded days go on and on
I feel I have lost and someone else won
I am so tired I am going to bed
Lay down for a while just rest my head

The media offends me it depresses me too
I need a break so I am counting on you
Give me some good news fill me with hope
Uplift me I beg you please help me to cope

BUILDING YOUR LIFE WITH A SOLID FOUNDATION

by Stephen Robert Sutton

You are building your life
With a solid foundation
Living your life
Without complication

Building your life
With a foundation of love
This is built
By your parent with love

They supply you with
Religion and truth
Starting you off
When you're in your youth

Their political view
Reflecting on you
All their morals
Will follow you too

When you grow up
You choose your own way
And in your life
You hear what they say

Often, we learn from
Our mistakes everyday
But we get through our life
In our own special way

HELPLESS

by Stephen Robert Sutton

I fell to the floor
Right next to the door
I had trouble getting up
And all I could feel was helpless

I fell down the stairs
And landed on the ground
Hurt my side
But didn't make a sound
But I was helpless

It's a well-known fact
Many people have falls
Tripping over feet
And bouncing off walls
They are helpless

People in the park
And people in the street
Like homeless people
Those we often meet
Are helpless

FADED LIGHT

by Stephen Robert Sutton

Like a faded light
You appeared to me
With a boastful grin
Fading into iniquity

But your sins will get you
In the end
Like meeting
A long-lost friend

Like a fading light
You came to be
A subject for
Controversy

This fading light
Is going out
And provide such answers
For those in doubt

Your religion
Will never save the day
Your thoughts will
Just simply fade away

PSYCHIC
by Stephen Robert Sutton

What do you see?
Through your special eye
An explanation
A reason why

The spirits seek you
To speak or chat
A psychic or clairvoyant
Where you are sat

Gifted with powers
To see what is to be
Unravel your life
Let us all see

The seat of a Wiseman
Dressed in dark clothes
Wearing tall spiky hats
And long hanging robes

You talk to the living
You talk to the dead
Some say its all happening
Others say it in your head

LIVING IN A BOX
by Stephen Robert Sutton

You live in the comfort
Of your very posh home
You will never be cold
You will never roam

While you enjoy all your food
Tuck into a roast
Discuss your income
Let's here you boast

So much rich living
Such comfort such ease
No one to think of
And no one to please

A man sits alone
His life in despair
No one to turn to
And no one to care

Cold dark nights in winter
Rain or even snow
With no one to turn to
No where to go

Living like an animal

Like a rabbit or fox

What life must be like

Living in a box

Plight of the homeless on the streets of Manchester

THE LOVE THAT NEVER WAS

by Stephen Robert Sutton

Like the flower that hardly blossoms
With a fragrance to admire
Or the fruit that just ripened
A taste you do desire

Like a sunset at the end of the day
This brings about the night
You dream about this moment
You live to see this sight

The one who is attractive
Is this the love that you desire?
The one that is so distant
Is she the one you admire?

Her eyes are blue and spark
Like diamonds in a ring
You want to tell her you love her
But you never do a thing

You love her soft complexion
Her hair of silk that does shine
You want to kiss her tender lips
To say she will be mine

But all you do is dream

And that is just because

She is with another man

She's the love that never was

PADDED CELL

by Stephen Robert Sutton

Listen to me scream
Listen to me shout
I am letting you know
That I am still about

Hitting all the walls
Swearing all the time
Bruising all my body
Isn't it a crime

I never knew what happened to me
I try to rationalise
Is it because I am mad
In this odd disguise

The madness is in my mind
Its started getting to me
Please get me out this padded cell
Come on set me free

WAKING BLIND

by Stephen Robert Sutton

The biggest shock to me
Happened when I couldn't see
I woke up blind one night
It was a dreadful fright

Not knowing what to do
What was I going through?
To this new life I appear
To live in mortal fear

No rhyme or reason I said
As I got out my bed
Reach out into dark new life
This is my horror it is my strife

Waking up to find I am blind
Or had I simply lost my mind
Stretching out my arms feeling for the wall
Frightened in case I had a fall

A teenager who had lost his sight
That was me and this was my plight
Not knowing how long it would last
Fortunately, it is all in my past

EXPOSURE TO LOVE

by Stephen Robert Sutton

Give me your thoughts
Make it your goal
Open up your mind
Expose your soul

Give me your love
Day after day
Help me to live
In my own way

Cleanse all my thoughts
Open my heart
Then I will know
We will never be apart

Kiss my lips
Oh, so tender
I love life
I live in splendour

I think about happiness
I think about love
I thank God
For my exposure of love

SENSELESS WORDS

by Stephen Robert Sutton

Voices drift
Within the air
People pass by
Without a care

Like an ever
Moving stream
It travels on
Like an endless dream

The sound does travel
On and on
And like the rain
Its come and gone

The words that leave you
Have been forgotten
Like unwanted food
That's gone rotten

The senseless words
Came from your mouth
They drifted north
And some drifted south

Carried forth
Within this time
They lost their purpose
As in a crime

Senseless words
Drift on and on
Never heard
Just by one

NAKED

by Stephen Robert Sutton

Stripped of my clothes
I sit naked in a room
A person with no purpose
Awaiting a pending doom

Vulnerable and alone
I remain naked on my bed
I reminisce my past
Thoughts within my head

Imprisoned by my past
In my naked state
Trying to keep my head
Considering my fate

I walk the street naked
Finally, I am free
I look at others
To see my own vulnerability

CALM WATERS

by Stephen Robert Sutton

Calm my heart

Lift my soul

Bring me close

Make me whole

Calm my waters

By the stream

Calm my storm

Within my dream

Trust me with you

Be my mate

Calm my waters

Before it's too late

A chilled out look at life in a tranquil setting far from the
hustle bustle of city life

FILL THE EARTH WITH PAGANS

there is a question
with an answer
that everybody's knowing
and that answer is
over seven billion
and growing
no need to count
it is official
so there can be no doubt

our Earth is over encumbered
by us useless eaters
over numbered
is the human race
a fact accepted
we see it for ourselves
and are told by teachers
no stats to leave repeaters

By Stephen Wright

THOSE EYES

by Stephen Robert Sutton

Those eye that sparkle
Oh, so bright
Those eyes that light up
In the night

Those eyes that tell
What you see
Those eyes which express
The inner me

Those eyes that age
And fade away
Those eyes that
Have seen a better day

Those eyes that tell me
I am still whole
Those eyes are
My very soul

Those eyes that say
I do
Those eyes that say
I love you

PROFOUND THOUGHTS

by Stephen Robert Sutton

Deeply my thoughts are
A philosopher you see
Coping with life
With my degree

With my conviction
My obsession to study
I take my time
I am never in a hurry

My analysis is detailed
Examine the truth
A time for tutorial
While I am in my youth

By my motivation
Self evident I found
Constantly striving
Completely profound

Profound is my name
Because of my thinking you see
Striving to improve
A scholar I shall be

FREEDOM FROM BONDAGE

by Stephen Robert Sutton

I live my life totally free

But ask me where I want to be

Back in time just to see

The dreadful time of slavery

I would take an arm

Of the best fighting me

And rescue such slaves

And free all of them

Seeing the cruelty

Of the British Empire race

Wasn't it awful?

A total disgrace

They took from the country

And boasted with such hypocrisy

We would strip them of rank

And set the slaves free

It was a mockery

History clearly defines

And yet they were glorified

Or so history finds

Now we do find

The message is clear

Black lives matter

This we must cheer

AFRICA

By Francis H Powell

I have never been to India

but I feel like I have breathed

in the air, conversing with a maharaja

While on an elephant sozzled with gin

I have pranced on a delicate leaf

Written poems and shaved my head

I have never thrown a rotten tomato

at a politician on a podium

Or carrots at an insolent donkey.

Nor have I run with a pack of hyenas

Or counted up all my misdemeanors.

I have always painted with a fullness of heart

And respected others despite divisions

My mind has drifted to Africa, and dust filled Somalia

I have shivered in Siberia and sweated in Egypt.

When I depart this world,

My head will be filled with memories

Of places and people strange and different

GOODBYE AFRICA

Goodbye my friend,

Thank you for birthing me and in doing so, you birthed my
divine.

You will always be part of me,

And in every way possible I will call to you.

From far and beyond, through fingers that may tremble,

I will raise my hands and release to you my love.

Think of me Africa.

In every glorious sunset, and when you send your rain,

know that I too am refreshed.

Oh how I shall miss your smell of dusty earth my beautiful
friend.

When the eagles cry and the baobab trees rustle their leaves
in response,

I too will sing in harmony.

When I run on new lands and swim in unfamiliar oceans,

 they will feel the very pulse of a land within me so great,

That I fear the waters may just part.

People will observe where I walk,

and see my footprints shadowed by elephants and more and
know,

That I have been one with the most sacred part of God.

I have slept in the very crevice of Gods heart,

And played in the earths most spectacular playground.

When I return, promise me that you will send me a hail
storm,

And shower me with the essence of you.

My beautiful, beautiful.

Untamed Africa.

Kate Clayton

@rubykatepoetry

Kate grew up in Africa and now lives in New Zealand, she told me she loved Africa the scenery was breathtaking and that she found their was a lot going on there. She loved the wild life and writes passionately about the country

IMMIGRANT GIRL

Never before had she felt such trepidation,

No map could prepare her for this brave navigation.

To leave all She has, and all that She knows.

To find Her own truth and to then call it Her home.

To shelve Her dreams and bury Her plans,

As She embarks on this journey and discovers new lands.

She folds in her belongings, Her face rather militant,

The space that once stood a girl, now features an immigrant.

Kate Clayton

@rubykatepoetry

THE DARKEST OF DAYS

by Stephen Robert Sutton

I worship my love
And her wildest of ways
To lose her you see
Would be the darkest of days

She determines my thoughts
And rules my life
But never the less
She is my wife

Whatever she does
However, she feels
Her every action
Always appeals

When I lost my heart
To that woman you see
I let it be known
I was as happy as can be

And now at her grave
I think of her ways
This is the worst time
The darkest of days

COURAGE

by Stephen Robert Sutton

I live my life
Without any shame
I lived my life
And played the game

I loved and laughed
My whole life through
And kept my cool
With so much to do

I was brave
In a times of concern
In living my life
With lessons to learn

My courage is there
for all to see
Through life's great battles
I came to be

Courage is shared
by a woman or a man
Whoever is like this?
I am their fan

Be it a man or woman

Their story is told

All of their life

Begins to unfold

SILENT WORLD

by Stephen Robert Sutton

No one knows
The way I feel
But in my world
You know its real

The silent world
I live my days
Without a sound
These are my ways

To see mouths move
Without a sound
Cars and buses
Moving all around

The birds are singing
Dogs bark out loud
Living in my silent world
Is really profound

I miss such a lot
Not hearing at all
I can't hear the clock
Ticking on the wall

We take for granted

What we hear and see

But just for a time

Please think of me

MULTI COLOURS

by Stephen Robert Sutton

I live my life in multi colours

May I explain to you

Like red yellow and green

Sometimes I feel blue

Multi colours explain the world

Like our society

Many colours like a rainbow

With so much variety

Colours are very useful

They describe my personality within

Often what I wear each day

Reflects the me within

Take the colour green

Like leaves upon a tree

We think of those who have the best

And are green with envy

The colour black is darkness

And white is so pure

Yellow is like yoke

A colour to endure

Red is for danger

So, I heard it said

So, take heed if you wear this colour

For it is you that they must dread

HOME BEFORE DARK

by Stephen Robert Sutton

I end my day at work
Time is getting on
I think about hours
Daylight will soon be gone

I race down the street
With my briefcase in my hand
Never stop to think
As I race right past the grand

I rush to the station
Running up the ramp
Donating all my change
To the homeless or a tramp

Rushing to the train
With the ticket in my hand
Dropped it on the platform
Where is it going to land?

I reach my destination
Hearing the dogs bark
I am glad I am back safely
Home before dark

FADED LIGHT

by Stephen Robert Sutton

Like a faded light
You appeared to me
With a boastful grin
Fading into iniquity

But your sins will get you
In the end
Like meeting
A long-lost friend

Like a fading light
You came to be
A subject for
Controversy

This fading light
Is going out
And provide such answers
For those in doubt

Your religion
Will never save the day
Your thoughts will
Just simply fade away

PORTRAIT OF MY SOUL

by Stephen Robert Sutton

Paint a picture
On canvas for me
Using colours
That plainly I see

Dark colours of
Purple and grey
Depicting my mood
At the end of the day

Paint it in detail
Like a good photograph
Don't make it funny
Don't make me laugh

Make it so dull
But clear enough to see
Paint me a portrait
Do this for me

You are painting my soul
This looks very real
Paint me a conscience
So, I can feel

Deep in my thoughts

I remember my pain

Scrub it all out

And start it again

RESCUE ME

by Stephen Robert Sutton

You reached out to me and pulled you out the mire

You poured water over me when you were on fire

You spoke to me when I was oh so low

You hurried me up when I was so slow

You calmed my waters cleansed my soul

I was so empty now I am whole

You instilled in me the chance of hope

Now I am so able to cope

You healed my cuts when I bled

You got some ice to cool my head

You fed me and gave me a drink

And when you spoke you made me think

Words of wisdom came from your mouth

As strong as the winds north and south

Gathers me up and whisks me away

Here I will fight another day

LIVING WITH A PHOBIA

by Stephen Robert Sutton

Rational fear is natural to us all
Like being on cliff top fearing to fall
Or falling in water thinking you would drown
Or on a ridge fright to jump down

But being frightened of a clown
Watching a show
Your friends want to see it
 But you just want to go

Frightened of a spider or a mouse
Or of noises in your house
What is this irrational fear?
What is this coming near

But phobias are real to you
Who can explain what to do?
Coping with your own mind
With no explanation to find

THE EFFECTS OF FEAR

by Demi Tilsley

It's not a living thing
It's not even there
But lives in our heads
It makes us aware

Stops us from doing
Minds no longer clear
Takes so much from us
The thing we call fear

It takes away our breath
Leaves us paralysed
A mask upon the face
Our identity disguised

Like the beat of a drum
Heart starts pounding
Everything closes in
The walls that are surrounding

Sweat trickles down your cheeks
Words start to stutter
Hands & feet trembling
Stomachs got a flutter

It will take over our life
A head full of regret
Improve the way we think
Reform our mindset

So don't hold back
Consequences are severe
Don't let it control you
The thing we call fear.

By Demi Tilsley

GRIEVING

I'm sitting there contemplating
My eyes filling up with tears
I remember all those memories
We shared over the years

As I lie there wide awake
I'm staring into space
The images in my head
Are of your beautiful face

I'm feeling empty, sad & lonely
Emotions I can't control
Feelings I've never had before
In my heart you've left a hole

Even though I know its true
They say that I am grieving
I cannot help the fact
That I am disbelieving

I'm feeling so hurt
Feeling angry deep inside
You couldn't possibly imagine
How many tears I've cried

They say that times a healer

That you will start to be okay
I know that is not the truth
Whichever year or day.

By Demi Tilsley

MY BRAVE GIRL (Gemma) by Stephen Robert Sutton

The front line nurses
Prepare for war
With PPEs and
Problems in store

Battling the virus
Day after day
Defying all odd
And with them we pray

There with them
Goes my brave girl
All equipped
And in a whirl

She bravely fights
The evil foe
With all the knowledge
Set to go

Her mind is set
To do her best
To comfort some
And cure the rest

MY PERFECT WOMAN

by Stephen Robert Sutton

Your eye sparkles
Like diamonds in the sky
Those show compassions
Whenever you cry

Your smile
Lights up your face
I feel secure when you're around
Never out of place

Your hair shines
And flows down below your neck
Your skin is smooth
And is clear without a speck

You are so warm
And comfort me from the start
I feel you with me
Even when we are apart

You are so clever
Oh, so very smart
I feel you with me
Close within my heart

HOPELESS MESS

What sense is there?
In clouding your mind?
By destroying yourself,
Are you so blind?

You consume
Such stuff in your head
By the time you are twenty
You will surely be dead

You pollute your body
And strain your brain
You live in a box
Close to a drain

You sit by the roadside
With your head in a bag
And manage a breath
Between each rolled up fag

You drink from a bottle
Shared by a few
But as for clear thinking
It's not up to you

Your dirty mouth

Keeps people away
You had better start living
In a new kind of way

Come out of that dustbin
You look such a mess
Change your image
And become a success

Dope will never help
You to find a job or career
But it will end your life
Within a year

Empty lives
Produce empty dreams
Shallow heads
Without any schemes

Wisdom belongs
To those who can think
Haggled brains
For those who can drink

So, wake up
When this nightmare ends
Who needs reality?
And who needs friends?

Logical thinking
Is far from your mind
Conquer your prison,
You are confined

You are a tramp
A modern day drop out
You are a mess
Of this I don't doubt

Your future died
When you were asleep
Now the frail weak body
Lies dead in a heap

MY FRIEND THE BOTTLE

Drink a glass
Of wine with me
Drink it down
Instead of tea

Drink a toast
to your lost friends
Have another
till the bottle ends

My friend the bottle
Is always by my side
My friend the bottle
Knows when to hide

My friend the bottle
Is close at hand
My friend the bottle
Is always in demand

So, drink
To my health
Drink
To my wealth
Drink
To the birth of a child

Drink
Until you're reckless and wild

Drink
To a new life to begin
Drink
Whiskey or even neat gin

But then stop,
Be in control
Don't lose your character
Or public role

Think of others
Who may get hurt?
Why roll in the gutter
Or even in dirt

Are you that desperate?
To sink so low?
Or have you the will power
To just say no

DIARY OF A TEENAGE DRUG ADDICT

I wake up this morning
With my hair in a mess
I can't help it
Oh, I couldn't care less

Yesterday was better
I don't know why
I feel dreadful
I just want to die

Just the other day
I had a dream
It was far out
I had to scream

A week a ago
I heard of a death
I have memories of her
It's all that's left

A single flower
Floats in a gutter
What a sad loss
Is all I can mutter

Cry after cry is all that I hear

From my hospital bed
Another mind is empty
Gone out of his head

THE SLUG THAT ATE MY LETTUCE

by Stephen Robert Sutton

A slug just ate my lettuce
What could this possibly be
He ate the whole dam thing
And I wanted it for tea

He polished off my lettuce
That greedy big fat slug
Gobbled it oh so quick
Like I knew he would

That slug must have a death wish
I said with a tut
As I lifted up my leg
And squashed it with my foot

I am only kidding
All life is sacred to me
I let my little fat friend go
And had something else for tea

THE BIDDY MOBILE

by Stephen Robert Sutton

Going shopping is such a nightmare

Normally I wouldn't care

I like to shop and see the sights

But let me tell you about my frights

For most I know it seems okay

They can go shop for most of the day

But for the elderly I have to say

In their biddy mobiles they like to play

Yes, mobile scooters are such a menace

I wish they would go to somewhere like Venice

Far away where they could do no harm

Let someone else have their biddy mobile charm

I dodge one and another comes along

Travelling past shops what could go wrong

I dodge another of those biddy mobiles

Then get caught under another one's wheel

They have stickers on the side of their scooter

Racing along and babbing their hooter

The sticker represents each person they hit

Every time they race past, I have a fit

One day it will be me who will be a statistic

Hit by a biddy mobile and crushed like a biscuit

The driver proudly puts a sticker on the side

You have no where to run and no where to hide

WALKING MY HAMSTER

by Stephen Robert Sutton

I wanted to walk my hamster

So, I asked my pet shops advice

He simply said how do you mean?

And oh, that's rather nice

I said do you have a lead

That's small enough to work

I read the expression on his face

Suggesting I was a burke

I have no lead that would be so small

He advised laughing up his sleeve

It was like I was telling a joke

About something he would not believe

I can offer you a ball he said

Holding it in his hand

I really don't think he can play

Anything not even on command

You put your Hamster inside it

He said explaining how it would go

It's so he can run around safely

This you need to know

And so, I felt more confident
As I took him to the park
He races around being chased by dog
And how they all did bark

Oh, how I was grateful for this ball
It really changed our life around
Looking for the word to express it
It surely is profound

CHILDHOOD STRESS

by Stephen Robert Sutton

Listen to my sorrow

Listen to pain

Watch my stress

Its happening again

My chest is wheezing

I am out of breath

People frighten me

Half to death

The asthma is with me

Causing me harm

I want stop it

It's causing me harm

I can't stop it

It's causing me stress

I am in a state

Yes, I am in a mess

So very worked up

I can hardly breathe now

Please tell me how to cope

Please show me how

No one understands
No one feels this way
I wonder how I make it
How I get through the day

I use inhalers
They stop this wheeze
With help from my parent
Who put me at ease

MANCHESTER AIR

by Stephen Robert Sutton

Arise arise to the Manchester air

Feeling free without a care

Breath it in within your skin

Just as you did when life did begin

All the races all of your kind

All your thoughts are brought to mind

Colour and creed are as one

Under the moon and under the sun

You working class have a place

All equal under Manchester's race

All alive and all do share

This our own Manchester air

We work together united in peace at this time

Live for a cause and don't commit any crime

And just as real as the stars above

We live for each other giving one love

Arise arise to the Manchester air

Feeling free without a care

Breath it in within your skin

Just as you did when life did begin

THE MANCHESTER BUSKER

by Stephen Robert Sutton

Standing alone in a street
Outside shops nice and neat
Playing guitar and singing out loud
She drew a very large crowd

The Manchester busker
As she became known
Performing for the crowd
Completely on her own

Her voice was heard down the street
Playing guitar tapping her feet
To the beat of a sound
People joined in all around

She played slow songs, fast songs
Rock and roll and rap songs
Reggae, blues and soul as well
Or ballads with a story to tell

The Manchester busker
As she became known
Performing for the crowd
Completely on her own

With her long dark hair

And a scarf round her neck flowing down

With a pair of ripped jeans

She played her way across the town

SAD MEAL

by Stephen Robert Sutton

To eat a meal quick
Fast food is a way
It's nice and cheap
And fills you for the day

If you buy a happy meal
You're sure to be glad
You're thankful for
All the food you had

But if you get a sad meal
You get an empty box
I would say you'll be lucky
If you found some smelly socks

A sad meal will never fill you
I just like to see you face
To find your meal missing
It's lost without a trace

Of course, I am only joking
Your meal is on the way
To see the look upon your face
It really made my day

LOVE WITHOUT BOUNDARY

by Stephen Robert Sutton

Love is not far away at sea

It' never distant as far as you see

Loves never lost in a forest or cave

Or lost in a tunnel or a thing you can't save

Love is the sacrifice that you can make

Love isn't false, love isn't fake

Love is without boundary

Without barriers no lines are drawn out

I know when I love I am never in doubt

Love is so happy it brightens my life

Love says I want you to be my wife

Love is positive it's what we strive for

Love is the opening of every door

Love has no boundary no beginning or end

Love is your soul mate love is your friend

Love comes from the heart I know that my friend

Love is forever and it is a god send

THE LIGHT OF DAY

I watch the sun rising
Shining on your hair
The way you walk
 Like you just don't care

Yet your voice keeps ringing out
Peace, I hear you say
Faded is your voice
By the light of day

I found you in my dreams
Walking in a cosmic heaven they say
But I will never forget you
By the light of day

So young and so good
Smelling like lavender they say
Shining like a beacon
By the light of day

Walking down the avenue
Strolling through a park
Making your presence known
Singing like a lark

I wonder when you will be with me

Present in my heart
Always together
And we will never be apart

I will love you forever
This is what I say
Under the moonlight
And through the light of day

DOUBLE EXPOSURE

In a castle away from the world
A ghostly place is there
With many scary happenings
Leaves you with despair

A game created to frighten you at night
Don't you want to join us on this plight?
Scary beyond much more that compare
Evident by the rising of your hair

But much can not be explained
Like missing bodies deaths occur
Like a Cluedo game life becomes a blur
Nothing is explained and nothing will ever be the same

TRUST CHARLOTTE

TRUST CHARLOTTE

S R SUTTON

Blonde girl from Manchester is free

Charlotte just comes to me

She is so powerful and alive

She knows just how to survive

By her beauty and her grace,

she lives on

Using her charm, she has won

Trust Charlotte to trek around the world so well

Trust Charlotte to love and never tell

Trust Charlotte for being foolish and rash

Always rushing and forever in a dash

Trust Charlotte for being sentimental and wise

See the love there that's always in her eyes

Trust Charlotte for her trickery and games

Don't trust her or you'll go up in flames

JOHN LENNON THE LEGEND

A man that was meant to be
A raw voice singing energy
Spilling out such melody
Like the man you were meant to be

Singing of love and romance
While you cry out peace rants
People listening when you talk
And many follow you when you walk

Your songs have such meaningful words to me
Speaking of oppression and when we are free
His hate and his anger of war in his day
Could only reflect on others this way

Rock and roll hero
A legend to me
A working-class hero
Is something to be
All of his mind games imagine them today
Winston O'Boogie
Is a legend today

SOLDIER

Here the war cries of many men
Going to war and back again
So proud of his uniform
His stripes and his colours
Shining black boots just like the others

Soldier protects all those of his kind
To live so securely for peace of mind
Patrolling the jungle patrolling the land
Protecting the child take hold of her hand

The army does not discriminate colour or kind
Female soldiers can have peace of mind
The female soldier stands proud as one of the team
They reign over all they are supreme

The soldier is proud and humble too
They fight with courage just to get through
A soldier is trained to survive everywhere
But they learn about compassion and how to care

DEEP IN THOUGHT

By the expression on your face
Your mind is in another place
A place that is distant like the stars
For all I know it could be Mars

In the deepest cavities of your mind
Who will know what you will find
The deepest thoughts, hope and schemes
Solving puzzles or analyzing dreams

Searching for answers of mysteries today
Holding onto thoughts or visions this day
Even more riddles enter your head
That seem accumulate when you're in your bed

ENDURANCE

Do your best in all you do
And do it well, it's up to you
You can be anything that you want to be
Just make the effort and you will see

Take all the steps and deal with the hate
Climb up the ladder and open the gate
No matter what your disability may be
You will endure it, just wait and see

Be ever positive and what you've got
In order to achieve this, you will receive a lot
With years of endurance pain and endeavour
You will have a life of fun and absolute pleasure

BEING DIFFERENT

Walking and talking in your own style
Just being you and wearing a smile
Wearing the clothes that you want to wear
Living your life without a care

Just being different showing your worth
The only one of your kind walking this earth
Alone or with company you're not really fussed
Doing what you want that is a must

Just being different to those you're around
Just being there without making a sound
People love you or hate or find you strange
Or they accept you for you'll never change

IMAGES OF DAVID BOWIE

On with the make up and glitter too
Bowie is made up to entertain you
With Ziggy standing on the stage
Like a performer from another age

With his spiky long hair on show
And glittery suit he's ready to go
Singing songs of time and space
With make up on his face

His voice gives a distinctive sound
And helps to provide joy all around
Glam rock is a thing of this day
As the seventies gets under way

By the eighties Bowie changes his style
Although he carries a distinctive smile
His stage presence is one to admire
The suits are part of his attire
He writes the songs and plays the tune
Flies through space up to the moon
Surviving bad times with his life in tact
Bowie is a legend and that is a fact

THE STONE BRIDGE BY THE STREAM

As I walk over the old stone bridge over a stream
My heart aches and my eyes gleam
I see you watching me from close by
And realise you wanted to die

We walked hand in hand across that bridge
And into the woods so deep
And now I walk across that bridge
And think of you I begin to weep

Your ghost waits for me each day
And I can only stand there and pray
Pray I would be with you just like before
Holding your hand just like before

The sun rises as you stand waiting for me
On the old stone bridge by the wood
I feel lonely and my heart aches
I would join you if I could

But life is cruel and impossible for me
One day I will join you one day when I am free
DYSPRAXIA (It's just the way I am)

I make such excuse for the way I perform
But I have been like this since I was born

With no sense of direction or lack of control
Or not achieving or reaching my goal

I correct my steps so I don't fall
People laugh and make me small
I cannot even catch a ball
And when I walk, I am sure to fall

Some days are good some days I am bad
Sometimes I will curse sometimes I am glad
My brain tells me one thing my body says another
Why am I like this I must ask my mother

Which is my left hand, which is my right?
Should I go to school and end up in a fight?
My routine tends to vary according to my day
Should I concentrate no way I play
It just the way I am I tell myself
I wish I was an ornament sat on a shelf
Something to admire attractive and nice
But this is me with the luck of the dice

FAR AWAY GIRL

My days seem so misty and blue
Was it me that left or was it you?
My life is so strange and confused
I feel so rejected and abused
Coping with my life is a problem you see
Am I still in a prison? Or am I free
What will this world offer me now?
Who will I love, will we meet and how?
We were divided in difference you see
But I often think was it you or was it me
How can I possibly take all the blame?
Perhaps we were too much the same
My mind is causing me too much pain
Is it just me am I going insane
I have been lonely for much too long
Who could ever say too much is wrong
I try to understand more each day
But the past is so misty so far away
I once loved you that's all I can say
But now we are apart you are so far away

WAITING FOR YOU

I sit at home and wait for you to call

I am so confused I am writing on a wall

I have written your name a thousand times or more

I have written it right across the door

Tis foolish of me to think she will return

When living her life is really her concern

But I will sit here what more can I do

And spend my time thinking just of you

So, I wait at home just waiting for you

Surely our life together is not really through

I lost you many years ago

We were divided by differences you know

We grew apart over a short time to me

Now we are apart at least one of us is free

In my heart I want you I feel this yearn

Please be with me I want you to return

THOSE IN GRIEF

Wipe a tear from a mourning eye
And please remember I wanted to die
My life seemed to last so many years
So don't cry don't shed any tears

Open your eyes raise your head
Its not your fault that I am dead
I loved you dearly with all my heart
So be not sad now we're apart

I drank to you my last farewell
And left you fresh flowers for you to smell
I left a rose pressed in a book
Near a verse, please take a look

I'm happy now I rest in peace
My painful body had to cease
Now at last I am free from pain
You are able to live again

THE LOST POET

The poet writes his final line
With his memory deep inside
Experience mixed within his dreams
With thoughts he could not hide

Hidden away in a fortress tower
So high upon a hill
Lost within his solitude
With dreams he could not forfill

A trapped talent within a cell
Within your mind fresh thoughts do dwell
A man that is trapped within his mind
Here the lost poet may dwell

Always thinking of the people, you create
When your asleep new dreams you motivate
Like a person within a person
Fictitious people within a dream
Nightmares make you awake
And no one will here you scream
The poet writes his final line
Of a person without a friend
The conclusion is written on this day
The poet must come to an end

So, daylight is over

Darkness will end the day

The candles are gone they burned so low

So, you must lose your way

And the dreams inside your mind have all gone

Just as the hot sun melts the snow

And as the winter disappears

You must leave this life and go

The poet writes his final line

With his memory deep inside

Experience mixed within his dreams

With thoughts he could not hide

Hidden away in a fortress tower

So high upon a hill

Lost within his solitude

With dreams he could not forfill

The poet writes his final line about things that couldn't be

Lived his life within a dream the poet writes his final line for
me

MY FRIEND THE BOTTLE

Drink a glass of wine with me
Drink it down instead of tea
Drink a toast to your lost friends
Have another till the bottle ends

My friend the bottle is always
by my side
My friend the bottle knows
when to hide
My friend the bottle is close at hand
My friend the bottle is always in demand

So, drink to my health
Drink to my wealth
Drink to the birth of a child
Drink until you're reckless and wild
Drink to a new life to begin
Drink whiskey or even neat gin

But then stop, be in control
Don't lose your character or public role
Think of others who may get hurt
Why roll in the gutter or even in dirt
Are you that desperate to sink so low?
Or have you the will power to just say no

DEPRESSION

In a dark place far from what I know
In a place so dismal where most fear to go
I linger alone far from my thoughts
Like a leper or a skin full of warts
Like a body disfigured by societies cruel tricks
I am in a bad way, I 'm in a fix
It's hard to explain my feelings you see
This isn't my way this isn't me
I don't eat in the day or show my face
I walk with my head down all over the place

Time passes by me I know not the hour
I am like a machine that has lost all its power
I go deeper and deeper in a dark pit
I don't care about life I don't give a shit
Without taking these pills I would surely be dead
Please help me escape from what lies ahead

BEING OLD

Take away the pressure
That comes of being old
And just leave me the pleasure
That's as pure to me as gold

Light a dozen candles
And watch me glow so bright
Each flame is like a memory
Remember me tonight

These wrinkles on my face
My hair is going grey
All that is left are my memories
Thoughts of yesterday

The songs I still remember
So clear from the start
But then my memories fail me
I forget the second part

FACING DESTINY

I feel at peace
Within my soul
Now at last
My mind is whole
For life's great pleasures are no longer mine
I no longer feel my body entwined
By problems of how I must be fed
Or how long will I sleep alone in my bed
I saw my destiny within my mind
I felt myself in ecstasy examining my find
So now I look up to you with my mind clear and bright
I look down on the world like a star shining light

AGAINST THE WIND

How weak I feel against the wind
That rages against me like a raging man
Forces me back so fierce
While I do what I can

With the strength of a bull
And as fast as a cheetah
Faster and fast but I beat you
Unbearably cold and pushed back with the rain
Harder and harder I can hardly explain

Bravely I battle its heartless gain
Getting wetter and wetter due to the rain
On and on I endure the pain within
Onward I go and finally win

GHOSTLY

Spirits of an evening rise
And you won't believe your eyes
As here before you crystal clear
Ghostly presence they come near

By chance within a haunted house
They appear and some do pounce
Restless souls linger through the night
And present themselves like an awesome sight

They haunt you in the dark of night
And make you jump giving you a fright
And to the break of dawn
You are startled to the morn

BE RULED BY ME

Don't ever let people
Tell you how to walk
Don't even let them
Tell you how to talk

Be your own person
You know you can
Do what you want to
Do what you can

Be independent
Take your own advice
Do what you want
As long as you're nice

Parents will guide you
Take hold of your hand
Try not to be lonely
But that's not a command
Be what you want to be
Hear what I say be ruled by me

BETRAYAL

In the dawning following the night

I will speak about a plight

The one we shall discuss

Is non other than Jesus

For what has come to be

Was foretold from history

From the scriptures old

This is what I was told

A man would be betrayed

His life would not be saved

A sacrifice he would make

Of his life god would take

He was to save mankind

That was on his father's mind

And so, the betrayal took place

When Judas kissed his masters face

Some may betray us this way

The example remains for us today

THEN CAME THE NIGHT

I love the day
To my only delight
I live out my day
Then came the night

My life fades away
When it is twilight
I leave the day
Then came the night

I give you my ears
I lose my sight
Its very clear
Then came the night

I have my dreams
Lost under starlight
I ended my days
Then came the night

THE OBSERVER

The observer sits and admires the view
He watches me and he watches you
He sees every move you make
He even observes the steps you take

He is never far with his watchful eye
He remains with you until you die
He observes every breath you take
And even observes every mistake

You cannot see this observer you see
Because he is invisible to you and me
But one thing is certain as life course you do take
He will always protect you and keep you safe
He has qualifications of a perfect man
And he has been here since life first began.

THE OBSERVER -PART TWO

Life is much greater than you and me
He controls the wind and the rain
And parted the sea

He observes the earth, moon and heavens above
He is so might so full of love
The observer created all things you see
From creatures on the land and those in the sea

His knowledge is great his mind is supreme
He even observes the things that we dream
He knows and loves you even when you are wrong
And when you're in trouble he will help you along
So, observe for yourself how he wants you to be
Then we can live in perfect harmony

THE BEGUILER

The beguiler deceives you with love and affection

He attacks you when you have no protection

He tries to fool and amuse

But he only knows how to abuse

With tricks and charms and acts of magic

The end result could be quite tragic

So, take heed of my warning and leave his arms

Take nothing from him, not even his charms

His beguilement is treacherous and cruel

His victim is often an innocent fool

Who knows nothing of beguilement, evil and hate?

Listen to me I beg you, before it's too late

Just think of goodness, drive him out of your mind

Reject his beguilement and true love you will find

THE JOURNEY

Hustle bustle everywhere
People travel without a care
On buses and trains, they have to go
On trams they travel too and fro

In crowded stations all day long
Delays in transport when things go wrong

All hunched up like peas in a pan
Filling the transport wherever they can

Sweaty bodies stand and sit
With bags and cases, they try to fit
Chatting some cursing wildly
Suffocating in such misery

Rude people push their way in a queue
With no manners except for a few
With the sound of children screaming so loud
Please rescue me get me out of this crowd

NOTHING IS REAL

In a world of imagination stood a man with frustration

A man that thought he was real you see

From a game was so unreal to me

He tried to make his way through life

He even invented a wife

And a fantasy woman as well

His life was a living hell

He couldn't even feel

He must have known nothing was real

The warnings were there before his eyes

So, listen and ignore their lies

It's written on walls and in the sand

So, you know just where you stand

You need to know what is exact

Nothing is real and that is a fact

ROSE

I watch you bloom into a flower
And laze away a midday hour
You seem to blossom right before my eyes
It was there and then I realise
That life is passing how very wise

You open all your petals in the sun
I know from this that life's just begun
I smell the fragrance of your bud
And life goes on as if it should

Throughout the summer warm and bright
You are a wonder a glorious sight
The days go by in their formation
And you remain in your location

The wind and rain come in force
Thrashing about without remorse
But you remain without surrender
My budding rose in all your splendour

SEA WAVES

The waves roll along a beach
Sparking under the sun
By the morn I see
That the day has just begun

Gently it flows across the sand
As clear as can be
With a faint whisper of a sound
All for us to see

So peaceful and flowing
It glides over the sand
Like the beat of my heart
Or the wave of my hand

Away from the chaos
The noise on the street
With the sea waves
Around my bare feet
Sea waves on the ocean
Sea waves on the sand
Moving to music and
The wave of my hand

BLANK CANVAS

Blank canvas waiting for me
I wonder what the artist can see
A person an object something to do
I want to create a painting for you

Splashes of white, swirls of green
The best image that you've ever seen
All from my thought from my weird mind
All known images things of this kind

Colours have meaning like the words of a book
Just search around you please take a look
Like word from a poet on blank paper you know
Follow my guidance just have a go

Painting by mood colours so dark
Dim is your vision you left your mark
Painting so bright show your display
This is his best work I hear them say

 The blank canvas begins a journey you see
A fine creation for you and me
Thinking of colours, I think of red
Now it is completed its time for bed

LEGENDS

Legends are actors
Part of the screen
Legends are rock stars
Part of the scene

Legends can be ancient
Part of history
Legends are men and women
Read it and see

Legends are made
From the talent they posses
Legends are from greatness
The fruit of success

Being part of a legend
Is part of the game
Being successful
Remember their name

Its about gifts and talent
That you present at the door
People love what you do
And ask for an encore

ACTION HERO

I want to be an action hero
So, I can stop kids bullying me
Brave like an action hero
And walk around totally free

In my dreams I am an action hero
Fighting my way through school
Walking around like an action hero
Instead of somebody's fool

I want to be an action hero
Playing in the school yard
Fighting off all the bullies
Making out to be hard

My life in school at present
Is being pushed against the wall
But my life as an action hero
I have the power to conquer all

NEW YORK CITY

The statue of liberty stands so fine
The lady of the city is so divine
A gift from the French years ago
Here on an island right here on show

In central park we walk along
A busker stands singing a song
With street performers working away
They come along to brighten your day

Artists and singers perform to the crowd
Comics will have you laughing out loud
With tricks to astound you beyond believe
Lennon's memorial has you stricken with grief

Many performers you see at time square
Dressed in costumes just for a dare
Shows are on Broadway only the best
More fine performers on with the show
Prepared for their audience ready to go

Brooklyn is another island close by
With a shopping mall to try
Then theres long island a place to be
Living your life happy and free

New York is a city that stands on its own
With crowded streets and a life in the zone
With cars and buses noise on the street
People pass by us being discrete

Now at ground zero an Éire sight
The bodies of many lost in fright
One time trade centres stood in this place
Now there are fountains a memorial with grace

New York is known for its many stores
Like Macy's for clothes which you see on your tours
With toy shops and Apple stores this kind of thing
Some places sell jewellery plenty of bling

GIFTED

You may have talent you may have fame
People may know you and remember your name
People are gifted in some special way
By talking to other and having your say

They may be artistic painting so clear
Or drawing a portrait of someone quite near
Or by making crafts that are put on display
Selling their products or giving them away

True gifts are a treasure and fine they may be
Showing your talent for all to see
On television and in galleries on the internet
Or on You tube they say is the best

People with dyslexia are gifted you say
I am dyslexic so what can I say
Dyspraxics are gifted I heard it is so
I am dyspraxic so what do I know
Watch and observe is this so?
Have I a gift I wouldn't know
If you would like
You let me know

THE VISION

Am I hallucinating my minds confused
Did I take something I am so amused
Confused by my thoughts you see
About things that are meant to be

See and hearing strange things by day
Confused by voice what did they say
Dreaming strange dreams at night
Struggling through mud in a fight

Demons are with me I swear
Tossing me up in mid air
Battling spirits in a fire
While living my only desire

Fading in images of my past
Visions pass my eyes so fast
Like the fast motion of a bus or a train
Something's got hold of my brain
How can I tell you how do I explain
It's very likely I am going insane

TIME

Time ticks like a clock on the wall
Time passes for you to recall
Forward it goes through the hours of the day
While the children in the schoolyard do play

Ticking away like the sound of a grandfather clock
Each hour chime sounds and the pendulum does rock
Time is your enemy time is your friend
Where did time go when you meet your end

SCOTLAND

Through mountains and glen whispering sound
The highlands of Scotland with views all around
Whispering Gaelic, the language of some
The sound of a bagpipe or the sound of a drum

The castles are many as plain as can be
Those mountains are calling come on to me
The stream of clear water flow through valleys so wide
Scotland's own beauty a place full of pride

Your winters are harsh your summers so grand
The sight of the heather grows wild in this land
The wind that blows southward can make a man freeze
And all of that walking brings you to your knees

With whiskey inside you warming your heart
And the love of dear Scotland with you from the start
Give me your haggis give me short bread
But no more whiskey because it's gone to my head

SHADOWS

Shadows follow me everywhere
I turn around and there is one of them there
Shadows attached to my body so well
They linger round me like a bad smell

Shadows are big and shadows are small
You never can tell where they may fall
They follow you here they follow you there
They won't desert you so never despair

Shadows are seen on pavement or walls
From the shining of light, the shadow falls
Dark as the night it will come again soon
By a night lamp or the light of the moon

All the shadows on the wall
Lots of images big and small
For yours will follow you around
And move about without a sound

LIFE IN A JAR

This is a prison of life's long pain
As for the meaning let me explain
People suffer from anxiety and fame
Some are blind, deaf and some are lame
Without all these things they would go very far
Until this time they must live in a jar

Fame restricts you from the freedom to move
Make plans for the future that they disapprove
A clear direct guided by fools around
Controlled like a robot without any sound
You live every day in a jar
A lost identity you don't know who you are

The title is ambiguous as you can see
But it expresses all things to me
Whether you are ill or just a star
Just remember you live in a jar
Who said your world is an oyster expression like that
Must have been crazy or some sort of Pratt

LIFES FIRST BREATH

Echoes of laughter
Or cups of joy
The beginning of life
For a girl or a boy
A wonderful moment
You can clearly see
From the very start
Of wonders to be
From life's first breath
Or the first beat of the heart
With close companions
Who will never depart
For trial and error
Will teach us the way
Learn from our mistakes
From day to day

MOTHER

Comfort me open your heart

And remember me when we are apart

You gave birth to me though I cannot remember

On a winters day deep in December

As I grew up, we came closer together

Our bond of unity lasts forever and ever

The closer I get the more that I feel

Is it a dream? No, it's certainly real

You comfort me when I am wounded inside

You shelter me when I have nowhere to hide

I treasure these memories like playing in the sand

Or country walks holding your hand

I like Sunday meals and all that you cook

Those bedtime stories that you read from a book

Mother stay with me here what I say

Don't ever leave me until your dying day

PROGRESS OF A FOOL

From a bastard child you begin to grow

Learned all the things you needed to know

About how to steal a loaf of bread

And forget all the things your mother had said

You knew how to hate, you knew how to lie

Take the path of fate and know how to die

Death and destruction you brought on yourself

By treading on others to gain your own wealth

So, die like a fool, for here is your end

You will die alone and without a friend

Even yourself you begin to hate

Showing your feeling now it's too late

Your dying hour, others will never forget

They were right, they won they're bet

They said you would regret the things you have done

And as you die a new life begun

For as one life ends another will start

Let's hope they are better with warmth in their heart.

CASTLES FOR KINGS, DUNGOENS OF THE MIND

Listen to my voice as it wastes away the hours
Talking about senseless things, like wizards and lizards
Trapped within towers
What pointless words I speak on this very day
And hope that you hear them, though you are far away
My mind is so confused with thoughts and wild things
Of jesters, knights of queens and kings
Oh, what waste less hours, what a pointless day
What a boring life, that all I can say
Castles for kings, dungeons of the mind
I feel so trapped here, I am helpless and blind
These chains are my bondages forever I fear
But when sunrise approaches, I still feel you near

DEVOTION

I sacrifice my life for you

I promise to be humble and true

All else I will set apart

And to you I give you my heart

With charity of mind, I devote myself to you

Please observe I am humble and true

You and I will surely understand

That is why I ask for you hand

That we may be one from this day

And let everyone witness what we say

Our vows to be humble and true

You will love only me and I will love only you

And by our devotion we will strive to be

In perfect loving harmony

For richer for poorer better or worse

Join hands and hope that our love lasts the course

No one will divide us our strength shall remain

Listen to my word as I speak so plain

As sure as the ocean will never part

I give my devotion and my heart

WHO CARES

Who cares about the problems that occurs everyday?

Who cares about the poverty or the pressures of the day?

Who cares about the starving people when riches are your gain?

Who cares about the unemployed I ask you once again

Who cares about the lonely who need some company?

Who cares about the hungry when you wonder what's for tea

Who cares about the young who are growing everyday?

Who cares about their future or when they are going to play?

Who cares about the old when they are frail and weak?

Who care about the humble who cares about the meek?

FAR AWAY GIRL

My days seem so misty and blue
Was it me that left or was it you?
My life is so strange and confused
I feel so rejected and abused
Coping with my life is a problem you see
Am I still in a prison? Or am I free
What will this world offer me now?
Who will I love, will we meet and how?
We were divided in difference you see
But I often think was it you or was it me
How can I possibly take all the blame?
Perhaps we were too much the same
My mind is causing me too much pain
Is it just me am I going insane
I have been lonely for much too long
Who could ever say too much is wrong
I try to understand more each day
But the past is so misty so far away
I once loved you that's all I can say
But now we are apart you are so far away

WAITING FOR YOU

I sit at home and wait for you to call
I am so confused I am writing on a wall
I have written your name a thousand times or more
I have written it right across the door
Tis foolish of me to think she will return
When living her life is really her concern
But I will sit here what more can I do
And spend my time thinking just of you
So, I wait at home just waiting for you
Surely our life together is not really through
I lost you many years ago
We were divided by differences you know
We grew apart over a short time to me
Now we are apart at least one of us is free
In my heart I want you I feel this yearn
Please be with me I want you to return

THOSE IN GRIEF

Wipe a tear from a mourning eye
And please remember I wanted to die
My life seemed to last so many years
So don't cry don't shed any tears

Open your eyes raise your head
Its not your fault that I am dead
I loved you dearly with all my heart
So be not sad now we're apart

I drank to you my last farewell
And left you fresh flowers for you to smell
I left a rose pressed in a book
Near a verse, please take a look

I'm happy now I rest in peace
My painful body had to cease
Now at last I am free from pain
You are able to live again

THE LOST POET

The poet writes his final line
With his memory deep inside
Experience mixed within his dreams
With thoughts he could not hide

Hidden away in a fortress tower
So high upon a hill
Lost within his solitude
With dreams he could not forfill

A trapped talent within a cell
Within your mind fresh thoughts do dwell
A man that is trapped within his mind
Here the lost poet may dwell

Always thinking of the people, you create
When your asleep new dreams you motivate
Like a person within a person
Fictitious people within a dream
Nightmares make you awake
And no one will here you scream

The poet writes his final line
Of a person without a friend
The conclusion is written on this day
The poet must come to an end

So, daylight is over

Darkness will end the day

The candles are gone they burned so low

So, you must lose your way

And the dreams inside your mind have all gone

Just as the hot sun melts the snow

And as the winter disappears

You must leave this life and go

The poet writes his final line

With his memory deep inside

Experience mixed within his dreams

With thoughts he could not hide

Hidden away in a fortress tower

So high upon a hill

Lost within his solitude

With dreams he could not forfill

The poet writes his final line about things that couldn't be

Lived his life within a dream the poet writes his final line for

me

MY FRIEND THE BOTTLE

Drink a glass of wine with me
Drink it down instead of tea
Drink a toast to your lost friends
Have another till the bottle ends

My friend the bottle is always by my side
My friend the bottle knows when to hide
My friend the bottle is close at hand
My friend the bottle is always in demand

So, drink to my health
Drink to my wealth
Drink to the birth of a child
Drink until you're reckless and wild
Drink to a new life to begin
Drink whiskey or even neat gin

But then stop, be in control
Don't lose your character or public role
Think of others who may get hurt
Why roll in the gutter or even in dirt
Are you that desperate to sink so low?
Or have you the will power to just say no

CRACKED PORCELAIN

ACTS OF ABUSE   S R SUTTON

CRACKED PORCELAIN

You were just like porcelain to me
With smooth skin perfect as can be
I kept you clean and free from flaws
Like my ornaments I kept you indoors
The image that I had of you
Was perfection and love that grew

But then my porcelain mask had gone
The colourful image that once shone
Defiled by others with a shameless grin
You had become cracked porcelain

Once you had been a model child
Now you are just crazy and wild
I nurtured a victim of child abuse
Now I could never let my daughter loose

The world turned its back on your beautiful face
Leaving you in such a disgrace
Defiled by others with a shameless grin
Now I know your cracked porcelain

DEPRESSION

In a dark place far from what I know
In a place so dismal where most fear to go
I linger alone far from my thoughts
Like a leper or a skin full of warts
Like a body disfigured by societies cruel tricks
I am in a bad way, I 'm in a fix
It's hard to explain my feelings you see
This isn't my way this isn't me
I don't eat in the day or show my face
I walk with my head down all over the place

Time passes by me I know not the hour
I am like a machine that has lost all its power
I go deeper and deeper in a dark pit
I don't care about life I don't give a shit
Without taking these pills I would surely be dead
Please help me escape from what lies ahead

BEING OLD

Take away the pressure
That comes of being old
And just leave me the pleasure
That's as pure to me as gold

Light a dozen candles
And watch me glow so bright
Each flame is like a memory
Remember me tonight

These wrinkles on my face
My hair is going grey
All that is left are my memories
Thoughts of yesterday

The songs I still remember
So clear from the start
But then my memories fail me
I forget the second part

FACING DESTINY

I feel at peace
Within my soul
Now at last
My mind is whole
For life's great pleasures are no longer mine
I no longer feel my body entwined
By problems of how I must be fed
Or how long will I sleep alone in my bed
I saw my destiny within my mind
I felt myself in ecstasy examining my find
So now I look up to you with my mind clear and bright
I look down on the world like a star shining light

THE CURSED

THE CURSED

Spirits of the past do see
A curse on a family
Mirrors just to see through
Like a gateway they come for you

Snakes, spiders and creatures come
To menace you when the curse begun
Voices crying out in fear
Touching you when they are near

Swamps devour you when you wake
Waters drown you in a lake
Fire consumes you in this hour
Or poison to your lips so sour

Deadly is the curse at night
You wake up screaming with a fright
Who knows what terror lies within?
As the mirror reveals its mighty Sin

WITCHES

WITCHES

Witches fly high in the air
Witches dance without a care
They cast their spells late at night
And dance around under the moonlight

Witches' cauldrons bubbling with the fire
They dance around and never tire
With cackling sounds, they make a fright
Like owls that hoot throughout the night

Witches display magic at night
What a display, an awesome sight
Trick after trick, spell after spell
An incredible sight didn't they do well

Dark witches are legends white witches too
Showing the world all, they can do
Halloween is the night for them
They can keep appearing again and again

EIGHT SKULLS OF TEVERSHAM

EIGHT SKULLS OF TEVERSHAM

This is a tale of witches
or a legend to me
Told of a family from
Teversham you see
The horrors and evil
which I will unfold
Of murderous dark
witches the story is told

The night when the witches evil did slay
Their wicked magic struck on their prey
Eight witches came forth into the night
Killed a young family who couldn't fight

A young boy called Eric swore revenge to them all
By forming an army and the witches would fall
Eight skulls were his trophy to hand to the mayor
Proof of their deaths that he must now share

Death to dark witches and descendants too
Eight more skulls he collected before he was through
But eight had a meaning that the witches new well
It means resurrection as part of a spell

So, the witches linger in a cave far away
In a place in Scotland that where they will stay

AGAINST THE WIND

How weak I feel against the wind
That rages against me like a raging man
Forces me back so fierce
While I do what I can

With the strength of a bull
And as fast as a cheetah
Faster and fast but I beat you
Unbearably cold and pushed back with the rain
Harder and harder I can hardly explain

Bravely I battle its heartless gain
Getting wetter and wetter due to the rain
On and on I endure the pain within
Onward I go and finally win

EMILY IN ECSTASY

Thoughts that a restless mind
An imagination of a different kind
Thoughts float like a stream in time
And travel along like an endless rhyme
Thinking of things, you used to say
Relaxing so peacefully at the end of the day

And like a sparrow in winter, you find a place to rest
To a place of solitude where you make your nest
You prepare yourself for each season to start
Ever more loving with warmth in your heart
But who is that woman people ask me
I reply its Emily who lives in ecstasy

GHOSTLY

Spirits of an evening rise
And you won't believe your eyes
As here before you crystal clear
Ghostly presence they come near

By chance within a haunted house
They appear and some do pounce
Restless souls linger through the night
And present themselves like an awesome sight

They haunt you in the dark of night
And make you jump giving you a fright
And to the break of dawn
You are startled to the morn

SIENNA THE VAMPIRE
BLOOD TRAIL-ACROSS TIME

Running through a forest fearful of
 her life
Sheltered by the trees at night
 in a dreadful strife
The vampire is alone hunted
like a dear
Running through the clearing
There she shall appear

Sheltered in a castle in a darkened room
There she finds a picture in which she is consumed
She falls out of the picture and lands upon a floor
Falls upon an observer close beside a door

This begins her story this is what's foretold
From out of a time portal in this time is told
A vampire from another age desperately seeking a friend
But what is her destiny what is written in the end

JUST LIKE MAGIC

It all began in Chantell's play room
one day
She heard the voice of a child as
she began to play
Alicia called out from her world
It was a call for help
Chantell's reaction was very clear
She let out a cry like a yelp

She entered a mirror into her world
Not knowing what I would find
To my surprise this other world
Had put me in a bind

A magic world, a fantasy world
Such a different place
With unicorns and witches
Amongst a different race

JUST LIKE MAGIC

SCARS

Be who you want to be
Do what you want to do
Live how you want to live
It's up to you

Forget what you need to forget
It's all in the past
Live for the present
It's with you at last

The scars do remind you
Of your past life that has been
Some scars are hidden
They will never be seen

Plan for your future
trips far ahead
But don't dream about them
You can't reach them from your bed

BE RULED BY ME

Don't ever let people
Tell you how to walk
Don't even let them
Tell you how to talk

Be your own person
You know you can
Do what you want to
Do what you can

Be independent
Take your own advice
Do what you want
As long as you're nice

Parents will guide you
Take hold of your hand
Try not to be lonely
But that's not a command
Be what you want to be
Hear what I say be ruled by me

BETRAYAL

In the dawning following the night

I will speak about a plight

The one we shall discuss

Is non other than Jesus

For what has come to be

Was foretold from history

From the scriptures old

This is what I was told

A man would be betrayed

His life would not be saved

A sacrifice he would make

Of his life god would take

He was to save mankind

That was on his father's mind

And so, the betrayal took place

When Judas kissed his masters face

Some may betray us this way

The example remains for us today

CADENCE

Please spare a little time
Just for my little rhyme
That dances on the page
And never seems to age
It has a cadence style
That travels all the while
It lightens up your day
Its nice in every way
Going up and down with sound
Like music all around
It is jolly it is fun
As bright as the sun
It warms and pleases
Without any diseases
Short and sweet
Unlike granddads feet
It smiles through the day
It is funny in every way
So, listen out loud
While it travels through a cloud
Then falls with the rain
How can I explain
Watch for yourself
Sitting on a shelf
And watch it fall
Getting very small
This is so
Now go

FALSE HOPE

Don't clutch at straws or live in false hope
You're just fooling yourself pretending to cope
With desires and pleasures far from your grasping fingers
Holding onto false hope until nothing lingers
You sit all alone with false hope till this day
Then years go by and your life fades away

Now you are aging you now see your mistake
You kept all your candles on a dream wedding cake
False hope was your downfall your cause has now failed
You're left alone in your life the ship has sailed
You stand at the harbour your boat sails in the distance
Now you remain in a lonely existence
So, you have learned a lesson don't try to cope
By dreams or by schemes don't live in false hope

MADAM McCAW

Madam McCaw is a dreadful bore
Who pries into your life
She talks and talks nags and nags
Take care she is never your wife

Madam McCaw she knows the law
She studies it every night
She stays up with you till the early hours
And she does this just for spite

Madam McCaw could be young or old
Who nags you to your grave
She could be watching you right now
So, make sure that you behave

LOVE ON THE DOLE

A strange romance is in the air

As you walk about without a care

For what is the point of feeling kind

For life is so empty and blind

For standing before you in a long queue

Is a beautiful girl looking at you

She seems so shy looks at you with a glance

So, you surprise her and ask for a dance

You take her to one side so no one can hear

And she blushes because you stand so near

Then you ask for a date

She replies this must be fate

Now you are successful you have reached your goal

This is a happy day its love on the dole

THEN CAME THE NIGHT

I love the day
To my only delight
I live out my day
Then came the night

My life fades away
When it is twilight
I leave the day
Then came the night

I give you my ears
I lose my sight
Its very clear
Then came the night

I have my dreams
Lost under starlight
I ended my days
Then came the night

IS THIS THE WAY I SHOULD FEEL?

Is this the way I should feel?
Is this the way I should feel?
When I argue in a room with paper thin walls
Run out of the room and slam all the doors
Is this the way I should feel?
I ask you
Is this the way I should feel?

When I love her so much but fear her touch
When she is so kind is it all in my mind?
Is this the way I should feel?
When life seems a joke and I laugh out loud
I know its unusual when I enter a crowd
Is this the way I should feel?
I ask you
Is this the way I should feel?

When someone tells lies
And I just close my eyes
Ignoring the fact
I know I should react
Or be ignorant or lazy
Be foolish or crazy
Dangerous or rich
Or fall down a ditch
And for get the entire world

Yes, why not forget this world
Is this the way I should feel?
I ask you
Is this the way I should feel?

JEREMY'S DREAM
(DREAM OF A DISABLED PERSON)

Come with me and journey a mind
Examine the facts and look at my find
Jeremy's dream is so complex and true
Think of it this way it could have been you

It began with a thought of reincarnation
A misunderstanding so much complication
Jeremy's past was very real
No one could explain the way he must feel

His handy cap prevents him from speaking
The only sound he can make is high pitched screeching
Who can explain? Nobody can
About Jeremy's past
As a near perfect man

KNOW YOUR WORTH

Can you value yourself?

Do you know your own worth?

Did you have a price tag?

Present at your own birth?

Have you been weighed?

To know your own worth

Balanced on scale like gold

Or the salt of the earth

Keep your price high

Balance things right

Be kind to all people

Be everyone's delight

Your qualifications are gathered

Over the years

So be confident at all times

Get rid of your fears

Your own personality

Is a qualification alone

Know your worth

You are one on your own

THE OBSERVER

The observer sits and admires the view
He watches me and he watches you
He sees every move you make
He even observes the steps you take

He is never far with his watchful eye
He remains with you until you die
He observes every breath you take
And even observes every mistake

You cannot see this observer you see
Because he is invisible to you and me
But one thing is certain as life course you do take
He will always protect you and keep you safe
He has qualifications of a perfect man
And he has been here since life first began.

THE OBSERVER -PART TWO

Life is much greater than you and me
He controls the wind and the rain
And parted the sea

He observes the earth, moon and heavens above
He is so might so full of love
The observer created all things you see
From creatures on the land and those in the sea

His knowledge is great his mind is supreme
He even observes the things that we dream
He knows and loves you even when you are wrong
And when you're in trouble he will help you along
So, observe for yourself how he wants you to be
Then we can live in perfect harmony

TAKE CARE

At the end of a letter
I take time to prepare
I reflect on the past
And sincerely say take care

When people part
For a journey they prepare
Their final words to their friend
Is take care

When lovers are parted
On a journey somewhere
They treasure their words
And say take care

Grand parents or children
Families with love in the air
Families reunite and just say take care

So read a nice letter with thought and with care
A cheerful letter that ends with take care

LAST CARESS

Gently the night came a red moonlit sky
I caught your tears as you began to cry
They flowed gently through my fingertips
Then into your mouth and moistened your lips

They failed to tell me of this time when we would be so close
About the pain and medication just an adequate dose
How I wish this last caress would last forever more
But life is hard and its now time to lose the one you adore
We talk about such silly things anything but death
Till she fell asleep in my arms and took her final breath

JUST ANOTHER MASQUERADE

I watch your face and your eyes do tell
The person within the odd outer shell
But deception may cause a person to fade
In a cunning masquerade

He conceals all the secrets to the depth of his past
And is joined by others like players well cast
A theatrical tableau is set before your eyes
It's a mass deception of cruelty and lies

They travel about from cities far and wide
With marvels around you with tricks on their side
So be wary of these who want to be paid
Its just another masquerade

DIARY OF A TEENAGE DRUG ADDICT

I wake up this morning with my hair in a mess
I can't help it oh I couldn't care less
Yesterday was better I don't know why
I feel dreadful I just want to die

Just the other day I had a dream
It was far out I had to scream
A week a ago I heard of a death
I have memories of her
It's all that's left
A single flower floats in a gutter
What a sad loss is all I can mutter

Cry after cry is all that I hear from my hospital bed
Another mind is empty gone out of his head
Pink red and orange is all I can see
Wont someone help me please set me free

LUCID LUCY

Lucid Lucy lean and juicy
Can you understand?
Why I love you naughty Lucy
May I hold your hand?

Lucid Lucy just eats muesli
For breakfast lunch and tea
Tell me Lucid Lucy will you marry me?

Lucid Lucy lean and juicy
Let me be your mate
Why shake your head Lucid Lucy
She tells me I am too late

ABSOLUTELY ABSTRACT

Paint a picture
and watch it glow
An abstract image
of a fantasy will grow
Images softly inter mingle
like mixed thoughts in a dream
Absolutely abstract
the best you have ever seen

With circles and stars that will never part
And fine white unicorns that will capture your heart
With dogs, cats and toads we even have mice
We even had spiders that didn't look very nice

Paint many pictures with triangles and squares
Now draw a building with plenty of stairs
Remember old Lowry he painted and then
Produced his likable match stalk men

Paint another picture even more bizarre
Made of odds and end taken from a car
Squares and circles shapes of a kind
Thoughts from elusions conjured up from your mind
Glasses and mirrors reflections of you
There are endless things an artist can do

MY LOQUACIOUS BIRD

My loquacious bird just likes to be heard
She sings her songs away
Though no one hears her she still wants to sing
All through the summer's day

My loquacious bird needs to be heard
Singing so plainly but clear
She knows how to find me and before long she is standing
near

My loquacious bird loves to be heard
She sits close beside me I dread
The only time she will shut up is when she's finally dead

MY CADAVEROUS WOMAN

Oh, woman of stone you stand alone
Unique in every way
Your cold and cruel I am so surprise
How do you get through the day

How I can tell I am in a living hell
Frustrated in every way
I pray to God for sanity to get me through the day
You look at me with a blank expression
Then drive me into a deep depression

For several years you have lived with me
Your only asset is making the tea
I try to survive and have to cope
You promise to leave and I live in hope
How do you get rid of an awful smell?
I dream of throwing her down a well
But fear the ghost that she may be
And just destroy my sanity
So, I live to face the day
My cadaverous woman is here to stay

THE BEGUILER

The beguiler deceives you with love and affection

He attacks you when you have no protection

He tries to fool and amuse

But he only knows how to abuse

With tricks and charms and acts of magic

The end result could be quite tragic

So, take heed of my warning and leave his arms

Take nothing from him, not even his charms

His beguilement is treacherous and cruel

His victim is often an innocent fool

Who knows nothing of beguilement, evil and hate?

Listen to me I beg you, before it's too late

Just think of goodness, drive him out of your mind

Reject his beguilement and true love you will find

TREE

How I wish that I were a tree
With lots of people admiring me
With lots of branches and leave to see
All adorned in my majesty

How I wish I were a tree
With the wind blowing through me
Waving about what a spectacle to see

How I wish I was a tree
What a sight I could be
Standing there for all to see
And no one to answer to just totally free

How I wish I were a tree
How profound that would be
Branches reaching to the sky
Dropping leave on those passing by
And the fruits that I bear
Falling apples everywhere
Or chestnuts dropping on the ground
Isn't it funny and so profound?
Oh, how happy I would be if was only a living tree

THE TREE

OUTSIDE THE JAR

Life in a jar was a protective zone
Where I lived my life all alone
With dyslexia and asthma keeping me company
Dealing with those now sets me free

Outside to jar is where I dwell
Having left a living hell
The jar was my prisoner I have to tell
From early life was there I fell

I learned to read and write myself
By choosing comics off a shelf
I discovered it was my place to be
By learning a new strategy

The asthma was caused by childhood stress
I could certainly see I was in a mess
I needed to change my state of mind
And leave my painful past behind

I struggled to be who I wanted to be
And now I live in ecstasy
Through education I excelled and now
I feel so overwhelmed as well

ELVIS

FOLLOWING THE KING

From a teen in the seventies
I discovered a man
With a fine voice
And I became a fan

They called him the king
Of a rock and roll age
As told by the media
Splashed on a front page

Elvis Presley was a legend
So, the papers say
His songs and his movies
Known to this day

I followed his life
From Tupelo to Graceland
I saw almost his entire home
And part of his land

I went to sun records
Followed his musical career

The foundation of his life
And felt him near

Graceland was wonderful

A fine place to see

But the best of the rooms

Was the jungle room for me

SCHOOL DAZE

Those days of being at school
Showing the teacher, I am no fool
Sat at a desk staring into space
Not being attentive and you could tell by my face

I wasn't listening my concentration was poor
All I wanted was to leave via the door
Art class was fun I could show off my talent and skill
I had a purpose, a role to forfill

Maths was my weakness fractions a chore
The teachers got frustrated they knew the score
I enjoyed English especially poetry
I enjoyed reciting verse it was fun for me

I liked history and French too
Domestic science and all that baloo
I hated being punished it was such a disgrace
Being hit with a ruler or slapped on my face

SCHOOL DAZE

THE JOURNEY

Hustle bustle everywhere
People travel without a care
On buses and trains, they have to go
On trams they travel too and fro

In crowded stations all day long
Delays in transport when things go wrong
All hunched up like peas in a pan
Filling the transport wherever they can

Sweaty bodies stand and sit
With bags and cases, they try to fit

Chatting some cursing wildly
Suffocating in such misery

Rude people push their way in a queue
With no manners except for a few
With the sound of children screaming so loud
Please rescue me get me out of this crowd

CALM WATERS

Calm my heart
Lift my soul
Bring me close
Make me whole

Calm my waters
By the stream
Calm my storm
Within my dream

Trust me with you
Be my mate
Calm my waters
Before it's too late

SHIELD MY LOVE

Shield me protect me
Comfort my soul
Love me forever
Make me your goal

Cushion my body
Shield my heart
Protect my body
Right from the start

Shield my love
Know how I am feeling
Love how I look
Its so appealing

Happy am I
Happy forever
Now you are with me
Please leave me never

PRISONER

The sentence is very clear
As in a court you do appear
The judge passes sentence in his own way
And you are condemned on this very day

Into prison you go unhappily along
Reflecting on your crime and what you did wrong
You are alone confined to a cell
This is your home now this is your hell

With mould and graffiti on the walls all around
Dirty and damp life is profound
For your deathly sentence lasts so long
This is your future it's where you belong

CRACKED PORCELAIN – KILLER QUEEN

I want to be like you
With long hair and eyes of blue
Though sometime your wear a frown
I just realised your eyes are brown

I admire your courage
And you are so free
How I wish I were you
Instead of me

I dress like you
Although I am a man
I walk like a woman
And I do what I can

I would kill for you
And protect your name
I am serious you see
This isn't a game

The people who die
Deserve all they get
I do it for you
To pay a great dept
I follow you
As you go out at night

And stay close by you
Keeping you in my sight

You were a victim
Of abuse in the past
They will not harm you
I will get them at last

I changed my body
To look like you
So many changes
I could be you

ANGEL OF LIGHT

by Stephen Robert Sutton

I watched you sleeping by my side
And calmly do you sleep
I hear you in the light of day
Gently do you weep

I watch you gazing out the window
With the light upon your face
So beautiful you look to me
You are so full of grace

Softly focused in the light
As pure as pure can be
Dressed in white I see you there
So clearly, I can see

My angel, do you think of me
As I do think of you
I think of you when I am lonely
I think of you when I feel blue

So, take my heart my angel
Comfort me at night
Guide me to my wonderland
Be my starring light

THE BEST AND WORST OF LIFE

by Stephen Robert Sutton

Picture the good times
As you live your life
Forget the bad times
They are full of strife

Treasure the moments
And capture the hour
Don't dwell on the past
And make your life sour

The moments that are good
Gathered from your past
Makes you feel happy
Forever they will last

Some serve as lessons
For you to learn from
Not all moment
But only some

Remember my words
Since life has begun
Life is for living
The best that you can

SOMEWHAT SUBDUED

I confess to myself
The way that I am
Life is intolerable
And such a sham

Existing at home
Hiding from a disease
Afraid of the virus
Frightened to sneeze

I am somewhat subdued
Feeling so strange
Hoping for a cure
And then life can change

Bitterness takes over
This incredible dread
Living an existence
I might as well be dead

But when I see the state
Then others are in
I look forward in hope
With a confident grin

RISK

We risk are life
In so many ways
By being alive in this world
And exist in a haze

The dangers you see
Are futile to some
The battles we have
And some of them won

We think with our head
But sometimes our heart
We consider the risks
Right from the start

We make decisions
Those are not always right
We make mistakes
And then get in a fight

CLOSE TO MY HEART

I have loved you
From the very start
You are part of me
Close to my heart

Your love astounds me
And makes me feel good
I think that I love you
The way that I should

Love has no boundaries
Open and pure
I love you madly
And there is no cure

I know that I love you
And we will never part
You are my loved one
Close to my heart

CREATURE OF HABIT

It should be noted
The way that I am
I am a creature of habit
And don't give a dam

I live my life fully
To my own gratification
Take care of myself
In any situation

Nobody rules me
I do as I please
Nothing will harm me
No stupid disease

I have a routine
That I follow to the letter
But I always strive
To do better and better

FUNDAMENTALLY SOUND

You are a unique person
This is what I have found
You're really quite a character
Fundamentally sound

I like you for your complexity
When you're with me it's ecstasy
You are the person meant for me
Fundamentally sound

You change just like a chameleon
By the way you are so reasoning
You fade into the background
And observe without a sound

Helping when you need to help
Your manner is exact
You want to be so versatile
This is a well-known fact

You are a unique person
This is what I have found
You're really quite a character
Fundamentally sound

MY SOUL IS YOUR SOUL STEPHEN SUTTON

My soul is your soul
My tears are your tears
And my fears
Are your fears

Since we became one
And are love had begun
My bed is your bed
Where we want to stay
My church is your church
Where we want to pray

My heart is your heart
Since we became one
My soul is your soul
Since we began

Your grave is my grave
That I visit everyday
My light is your light
That shines through the trees
With a whisper of your voice
Within a gentle breeze

I will always be with you
Part of your heart and soul

I live my life with you
This is my goal

I think of you each day
And what you mean to me
I cry out loud by your grave
Thinking of the life you gave

Please God set me free
Don't leave me in misery
Release me from captivity
Take the blindfold off me
So, I can clearly see

I don't want to moan
I don't want to live alone
Don't leave me in pain
Let's live together again

BELIEVE IN YOURSELF BY STEPHEN SUTTON

Be yourself that's all that matters
Don't let your life fall about in tatters
Consider your life as your very own
And ignore anyone else who choose to moan

Vacant minds who steel your thoughts
Who see imperfections and all of the warts
They don't give a toss for you or your friends
And grasp hold of life until it ends

So, believe in yourself in your own needs
In all that you do and all of your deeds
Learn how to love your very own self
And live in comfort with your own wealth

Your wealth is your happiness your very own gain
For money is nothing let me explain
You can have all your riches and be so sad
But life with self worth makes you so glad

THE ENEMY INSIDE
BY STEPHEN ROBERT SUTTON

Step inside my mind
Take a journey with me
And try to fathom out
Who I am meant to be

See who I am
Hiding in this shell
Experience a person
Living in this hell

Step inside this mind
Drift away with me
What is locked in my head?
Take a look and see

Who is this that lies within?
A tortured soul no doubt
A fragile person deep within
Or a person reaching out

Glance into my thoughts
Disturbing as they are
This is why I am distant
That why I am so far

What lurks within my mind?

It's the enemy inside

And no matter what I do

It always tries to hide

ABOUT ROB KRABBE

Rob Krabbe lives with his wife and family in a small town in the farm lands of Kansas. He moved there from Los Angeles, where he lived and worked from 50 years as a writer and songwriter, composer. He has published poetry, literature, and music of all styles, plus countless poems and songs. Rob spends his time doing what he's always done professionally, writing music and poetry. He even has published his first novel and has plans for a series.

Take Your Hair Down

A Poem by Rob Krabbe

I wanted to weep. There was
something about her eyes.
Something missing. Replaced
by something delicate, but tired
and resigned, like seeing the
reflection of God between the lines.
Her face, was like frail silk lace
laid gently on an old stained pillow.
Death notwithstanding,
her soul took the moment.
Grace earned, dying chaos,
above a fool's gaze, beyond
the need for any earthly reason.
This weathering dance of age,
the body, life and ebbing pulse,
softly; her spirit trembled like
a laying on of hands, ministering
toward the end.
Inside the forgetting, deep
within the madness,
she knew.
The reality; she couldn't
remember anything at all;
not even that there was
such a thing as remembering.

"Do I know you?"
she asked, traversing time to
when days, she knew, she was
to know, and a weak ghost of
a sly smile.
"Yes, grandma, you do."
There was a tortured question
burned into her eyes that kept
popping up like random
lightning bolts.
"I don't know what to do, what
am I supposed to do?" Panic and
angst, boiled between paper thin
skin and decaying trembling muscle,
almost tearing it open with every
spasm of fear.
"There is nothing more to do, Grandma,
rest now. You've done everything."
"You go to hell, get out!"
Sudden shrieking demon escaping.
I gulped a deep almost-breath
and grabbed her hand.
"What do I do?" she cried;
looking up with a child's
eyes, and weeping, "I just don't
know what I'm supposed to do."
"You look like Bobby."
Then a bird, landed on a windowsill

just outside her room.

Sudden smile, a tear forgotten,

but rolling down her cheek,

To her; gone and past,

and suddenly a thought jerked

free from the muck and mire.

"Robin red breast." she laughed,

a little school girl for a second.

Then dimming deep in a still

burning candle, almost out of

wick and wax, lightly touched,

this almost-afterlife as the end

wrapped her in pillows and

hospital blankets with the name

of the county faded on them

and the smell of what, ammonia?

"Mary?" she heard in the wind.

"Yes Bob?" my grandpa's name.

She was no longer with me,

as he leaned over to her,

brushed a delicate cheek

with his vaporous finger

and she smiled a familiar lover's smile.

There is an uncommon beauty in

70 years of love and shared life.

She smiled, hearing him again,

"Yes, we have had a long,

and good life my darling.

I must look a . . . sight."

She fluttered a bit, like the old days.

Grandma Mary took the

penultimate deep rattling breath

into her trembling body.

Then as if she heard him ask,

the question her memories expected,

"Yes, of course," she agreed,

and then smiling, "frisky man."

Now my own tears, of witness

to the precious and sacred moment.

My grandma, in her death bed,

reached back, and let loose

imagined long beautiful thick

brown hair.

"Oh you," she giggled,

as her remnants, thin and white

fell to the pillow, like fragile spider webs.

Then her hand,

after ninety-eight years,

gently, softly, found a resting place

near her face on the pillow

not needed anymore.

Her muscles all relaxed in turn,

one by one by one,

each one finished of purpose;

each one, done and done.

The slow exhale of a long life

as her lover took her once more
in her brain's last gasp, and light.
Grandpa Bob whisked her off to
eternity; her soul bursting forth
free from the now dead flesh,
as her hair clip fell to the floor
from her open hand.

© 2021 Rob Krabbe
NoonAtNig

The Night Bob Marley Died

© 2021 Rob Krabbe

I love the rain.
It heals me like carbon monoxide
gently lulls me to sleep.
It cleanses me of my fears.
I lay back, wearing only rain drops.
Counting them as they fall on my body.
Cooling my skin.
Rolling down my flesh.
Feeding the soft grass.
I enjoy a moment of purging tears.
My heart cries, sure, but in vain?
I've already been dead a thousand years.
Time comes and goes.
The Jesus Moon sails high.
The darkness caresses me,
rests me, tests me,
works its way into me,
into the melancholy.
My dreams, like quick sand, bring me low,
sneak me a vision of death giving life.
They try me, inspire me, but I don't bite.
Creation strokes my hair and
coaxes me there with sorrow for
all the things I'll never know.
Now I really want to go.

Dear middle of the country,

Kansas flatland.

Welcoming and sharing

the songs of Bob Marley.

Singing about love and hope.

I get that deeply.

Neatly, the groove, deep pockets,

lots of beautiful air in the arrangement.

Handing out hybrid blues,

and a kind of powerful derangement.

A band's blood,

playing your dues.

That pulsing slamming provision,

the soul's bed to lay down

the lyrics. The message. The words.

I hate words.

They cheat me.

Like now.

Redemption songs.

Life songs.

Blood had a sound,

Till the police showed up

and closed the club down.

Yes, they tried to kill Bob Marley in 1976.

That message, they had to fix.

Pressing down I, and lifting up the soul by

embossing care and compassion

upon the hearts of future healers.

Love breeds love. Lies breed politics.

Mile 235 gone.

I saw an old man, knees and

miles deep in an empty field.

Shovel in his hand, watching me.

Bob loved him smoke

and smoked him love.

They couldn't kill I,

but cancer could.

Then that was done.

I stopped the car.

The farmer man was gone, gone.

A craftsman, he.

A grave. Perfect spot.

Masterfully dug,

six feet deep.

"Nice hole." Says I to no one.

Then wanted I to die.

Thought to cut in line.

Beat the new tenet

to that beautiful grave.

They put my younger

brother in instead.

He was the first one dead.

I hit the highway again.

Some say the CIA killed Bob Marley

Buried him in a small grave

on the Kansas plain.

That's insane.

We struggle in this life.

Never promised an easy ride.

Nor farmers a drop of rain.

Or me, a great place to hide.

I'm pretty sure the voices I hear

are who I really am inside.

I knew that for certain,

The night Bob Marley Died.

EMPATHY
BY STEPHEN SUTTON

I cannot explain
But I feel everybody's pain
Everybody's grief
With everybody's tears
Everybody's sadness
And everybody's fears

I get this odd feeling
When you are around
When you are near me
Though you don't utter a sound

I feel a tingling
Right through to my bones
Like a clear signal
Without any zones

Like the warning of a car
When your too near a wall
Prevents you from crashing
It sounds out a call

Hark to my warning
Here I despair
I shall be with you
Because I do care

PECULIAR PEOPLE

BY STEPHEN SUTTON

In this world
We live with so many souls
With their own thought
And so many goals

With odd quaint faces
And particular dress
I don't understand
I found it odd, I must confess

With so much in mind
And thought of no other
So many odd thoughts
One after another

Peculiar people
Live in odd ways
Thinking strange thoughts
All through their days

Peculiar people
Wear peculiar clothes
Like t shirt and jumpers
Hole in their clothes

Extremely strange make up
And piercing in odd places
With strange looks
And such funny faces

But what is strange
I just must say
Who is a peculiar
Is really they

Why do we criticise
Give our opinion of them
Is it for us to comment
A voice to condemn

SANDS OF TIME

BY STEPHEN ROBERT SUTTON

Gently pours the sands of time
From the time glass pouring free
Slowing out the narrow gap
Clearly it seems to me

A way of measuring time
From hour to hour, it seems
Like the lingering course
Of all my personal dreams

It reminds me of time passing
All the past gone by
Like the waves of the ocean
Or a beach that's never dry

Happy moments seem to linger
As time begins to pass
Cherishing these memories
Like sand within the glass

ANXIETY HOLDS ME TIGHTLY

BY ELLA BRIGGS (AGED THIRTEEN)

Anxiety holds me tightly
It creeps it ever slightly
Sometimes it whispers
Sometimes it shouts

But it will not be heard
I believe I am strong
But how I am
So wrong
Self-doubt, negativity
And hurt to name a few,
The list is goes on
It's easy for anxiety to do
Punch me in the gut
Head constructs terrible thoughts
Stare into a mirror
And see my flaws
Disgusted and ashamed of my reflection
Anxiety through my eyes
And out through my mouth

Boss me around
Toss me without a care
Watch them unravel, I listen
Unable to take control

Anxiety holds power,

Insecurity runs deep

Permanent scars

No one can see

It presses on my chest

Unable to breath

But I remember

I am just stressed

It waits to creep in

Ever so slightly

My anxiety holds me tightly

MY ANXIETY

BY STEPHEN ROBERT SUTTON

I think of my anxiety
My feelings within
How, it affects me
Where do I begin

My heart beating faster
I am shaking with fear
I get so anxious
When people came near

I hate large crowds
Or closed in places
Frightening people with
Frowning faces

Feeling sad and slightly mad
Anticipation and so much frustration
A feeling of unease
When all I wanted to do
Is please
Please put me at ease
With my anxiety

GIRL WITH THE PURPLE HAIR

BY STEPHEN SUTTON

She seems free without a care
The girl with the purple hair
Her mind seemed far away
It's the way she preferred to play
The girl with purple hair

She acted out her part
Like someone who stole her heart
Seeming sad by some event
Like friend that came and went
For the girl with the purple hair

The girl likes to be unique
And dress in her own way
Like making a statement
Finding something important to say
The girl with the purple hair

Listen to her follow her advise
Don't stare at her
That's just not very nice
She has an opinion
That she would like to share
Its deep in her mind beneath her purple hair

LONELY

BY ELLA BRIGGS (2023)

I've known many kinds
of lonely during my life:
The definition of lonely
I'm sad lonely
I'm scared lonely
People lonely
Even song lonely
All these kinds of loneliness,
they float around aimlessly through my head
ever since I can remember. But only recently,
have I realised what true loneliness is
it's that feeling where you can't rely on anyone or anything
because it's not there for you anymore.
When your friends fade away,
your plays star to wither,
when it seems like no one cares about you
when all you have is yourself and nothing else.
That's what I think loneliness is…

THE CEMETERY

When life is gone
The spirit goes onward
The body enters the ground
People will mourn
Sombre are they
And tears are all around

Down the body to the ground
Lying in a pine bed
Their memories cease to exist
As no more tears they shed

You visit the grave
With fresh flowers in your hand
And speak fine words of comfort
that fall like grains of sand

Looking to the future
With memories at hand
Past memories are treasured
They were so grand

THE NIGHT SPEAKS OUT

BY STEPHEN SUTTON 2023

The night speaks out
But no one will see
It speaks of a house
That you may see

A place far from anywhere
Where few dare to dwell
A fearful place in the night
That's like a living hell

With its drafty window
And creaking stairs
A place like no other
Nothing compares
It has cobwebs and insects
A few running mice
If you stay for some time
You will surlily pay the price

LOVE EXPLAINED BY STEPHEN SUTTON

Love is as deep as the ocean
Love is as warm as the sun
Love is an unselfish act
When new romance has begun

Love is sacrificing to me
Love is as warm as can be
It flows like blood from the heart
And gives life that will never part

Love is no stranger
It is your friend
It should be with you
Right to the end

Love is so longing
To have you next to me
Love is so humble
Priceless and free

SABRINA

BY STEPHEN SUTTON 2023

Sabrina my darling I love you
Your eyes are sparking and bright
I feel you close beside me
From early morning until night

I feel your breath upon me
As you sleep away the night
I feel your heat beating
As soon it became daylight

Sabrina, I call out to you
Occasionally at night
Feeling you close to me
Makes me feel warm and bright

But my love I know that you left me
You passed away in your sleep
Whenever I think of you near me
Then I begin to wheep

MANEATER

BY STEPHEN SUTTON 2023

Look out for the maneater

She is always on the prowl

You can tell when she is coming

She lets out a growl

Man is her pray

As she hunts and claws them

She sneaks and she hides

Till finally kills them

She smells they are close

She can smell their fear

You won't know that she is close

Until she is near

She is cunning and wild

The worst of them all

She is able to kill you

With the power of her paw

RESPECT FOR OUR EARTH

We who dwell upon the earth
We have been here from our birth
Taking for granted what keeps us alive
Without the earth we would never survive

So, we should respect the earth
Give back to it for what it's worth
Not destroy the trees and the sky
That would surely be very unwise

To cause pollution in the air
This is considered very unfair
This earth was designed to cater for man
After all it where life had begun

The animals should be respected as well
Not be killed and they're bodies to sell
We must all love each other, living at ease
And protect all things even the trees

NATURE IS MY RELIGION

We worship God in our own way
This is how we get through the day
We speak to our god showing we care
When we are alone in our private prayer
People go to worship in a place to congregate
Considering they're future and very own fate
They call it Gods house according to belief
And often attend when they are in grief
But nature is my religion
The earth is my church
The tree is my resting place
Where the birds like to perch

Whatever I want
The earth will provide
Whatever I need
Nature is on my side

God bless the sea
And the rolling tides
So, I bless the earth
The nature it provides

CHASING DREAMS

Sometimes in my life
I dream of things ahead
I dream of these
While I am in my bed

I hope to be a writer
Writing fantasy
This would be so great
An ideal life for me

Living out my fantasies
Being who I want to be
Living in a fantasy world
Creating stories to see

Making up such characters
Heroes from my heart
Providing the reader with a shock
In the final part

THE BELLS RING OUT A WARNING

The bell rings out across the land
Somebody needs a helping hand
To ward away the devil's chime
An to prevent an endless crime

The evil spreads across the land
And give such treachery a helping hand
As death gives out its deathly blow
Who is next no one will know

But the bells sound out for all to fear
Here it is coming so near
For death will claim another soul
Catching you in its jaw
It will eat you whole

CREATIVITY

My creativity is like
The beating of a heart
Pumping life around the body
Giving life from the start

Sustaining life whenever it can
That life's ultimate plan
Reaching out to whoever is there
Hoping that someone will care
With word and picture
That tell their own tale
Give comfort and support
While love will prevail

LEGEND OF THE TIME WITCHES

BY STEPHEN ROBERT SUTTON

The witches are here
The witches are near
Protecting the earth
And the babies at birth

Thank God
For the land
For lending
A hand

To the souls
That are near
Without any
Fear

Casting their spell
In order to expel
All the bad that came
When the devil plays his game

Dark witches' rebel
And send souls to hell
But white witches are near
To expel all the fear

Time witches come forth

Using their spell

Sending them on

Straight back to hell

A SCOTTISH TALE

BY STEPHEN ROBERT SUTTON

In the northern highlands
Of Scotland goes the tale
Of a mountainous place
Where cave dwellers did prevail

The cave dwellers lived
And spent their days
Worship as druids
In their spiritual ways

Until came the night
When the moon was full
A sacrifice was needed
A sheep or a bull

The warriors were dividing
As a decision was made
As a human was chosen
A girl from the cave
Some said human sacrifice
Was against Gods plan
This was when
The fighting began

For despite the warning

Some conducted their plan

They made the Gods angry

And a storm from the sky began

Burning rocks

Came out of the sky

Raining upon them

And they wondered why

TIME PASSES

BY STEPHEN ROBERT SUTTON

A time to live
A time to die
A time for forgiveness
A time to cry

The ticking of a clock
Chiming sounds the hour
From an old-fashioned clock
Within an old clock tower
The ticking goes on
Sounding out the time
Then the old ticking clock
Sounds out a chime

Listen to that tick
Like a beating heart
Count out the rhythm
Right from the start

THE EXTREMES OF INCELS

BY STEPHEN SUTTON 2023

They are men who hate women
They prey on the female race
Why do they do this
Why do they have hatred in their face

They have no reason
 to hate
this is the curse
of their fate

rejected, betrayed
and abused
they are so wrong
and confused

women should be
respected and like
not abused, attacked
or strike

incels murder
in rage
this is part of
their outrage

WOMEN'S RIGHTS

BY STEPHEN SUTTON 2023

Women should be equal
It's how things ought to be
Standing next to man
That's my philosophy

Women have made good leaders
Back in history
Powerful strong women
This is what was to be

But women were also surprised
Made to feel second grade
Put in their place by men
Who wanted them to be obeyed

Suffragettes paved the way
By all their protests in the street
Chaining themselves to lamp posts
None giving in to defeat

Now they have a voice
Let the people know
We are here to stay
And will never go

STALKERS

BY STEPHEN SUTTON 2023

People who follow others
Obsessed with them so
In love with their lives
How far will they go

Photos of their victim
Appear all over their walls
Taken at random
When night time falls

Followed by day
And followed at night
Constantly observing
Until morning light

Terrorising their victims
By their obsession it's told
The persons in danger
What will unfold

No one is aware
Of the extremes they will go
But to stalk their victim
No one will know

IN MY WORLD

BY STEPHEN ROBERT SUTTON 2023

In my world nothing can touch me
In my world nobody cares
No criminal activity
Nothing compares

My world is a safe place
With wonders to see
No fear or resentment
Just let it be

I travel the mountains
Rivers and the sea
Being my own person
I am travelling free

My imagination is good
My fantasies are great
It's all in my world
Through a bright shining gate

GRANCARNA THE GREEN PLANET
BY STEPHEN ROBERT SUTTON

In a place within the universe
A planet did exist
Grancarna the green planet
The planet covered in mist

It was green gas around the planet
And the people were so green
Hostility did exist
Some people very mean

With Goblins, giants and witches
All very green
Making the world so different
Peaceful and serene

But the planet was in conflict
In a senseless war
The witches and the goblins
What did they have in store

But in the bloody conflict
Many people were to die
Until peace returned to Grancarna
From white witches from the sky

The time witches came to the rescue

Supporting those who are good

Bringing daylight from the darkness

Just like they knew they should

LIFE OF THE INCEL
BY STEPHEN ROBERT SUTTON

How sad am I?
That I am rejected
This is strange to me
And so unexpected

That women find me
So ugly you see
So dull and boring
How could this be

The chads in life
Have all the fun
He has all the wealth
Under the sun

The Stacy's in life
Are attracted to this
They live out their life
In perfect bliss

While the incel suffers
Left in the cold
We live out our lives
Lonely and old

I hate all the Stacy's
All the chads too
I feel so much hate
I could murder you

Incel is real
Why can't you see
What all the Stacy's
Are doing to me

I am full of sadness
And humiliation
So lonely and sad
Full of frustration

So, I took my own life
To get me out of this hell
Just one more statistic
Just one less incel

THE LOVE OF MUSIC
BY STEPHEN ROBERT SUTTON 2023

Music warms my soul
Music warms my blood
Like the rain from the sky
Until it begins to flood

Play a simple ballad
Write a stylish tune
Like a thousand melodies
Travelling to the moon

A with purposeful words
Playing in my head
With sound of a lullaby
Playing near my bed
This is my love of music
This is where it's at
The sound brings back memory
What do think of that

Travelling round the world
With music in my mind
Traveling on trains and buses
New places I do find

BE SAFE AT ALL TIMES

BY-- STEPHEN ROBERT SUTTON

Most of us are vulnerable
Nobody is safe
This is a true statement
Within the human race

Never be alone at night
Not at any rate
With the dangers on the street
That will your fate

Don't take that risk for any thing
It never is quite wise
Do not put yourself at harm
It will be your own demise

Women and men are vulnerable
At risk in every way
Don't take any chances
Take heed to what I say

DON'T LET THE LIGHT IN

BY STEPHEN ROBERT SUTTON 2023

Do not let the light in
Shining in the room
Leave me in the dark
As I am filled with gloom

I hide in the dark
I hide away my shame
I pretend it is not happening
All a futile game

Leave me to my feelings
Haunted by my past
Left with all my guilt
With dim memories that will last

I cry a million tears
But nothing helps my pain
I know one thing for sure
I am definitely going insane
I hold a knife in my hand
The blade cuts through my skin
The blood drips through my fingers
And my nightmares do begin

I swear I feel relief

As blood eases from my soul

I find my body resting

Now my life is whole

EMPIRE

BY STEPHEN ROBERT SUTTON 2023

Glorious it said to be
This empire that we claim to see
With all its spender of unclaimed land
And all supporters lend a hand

Across all nations it brags to be
But what a mockery it means to me
As in history books it looks so fine
And to the king it will shine

Praised by the government for showing the way
And I go on reading what they say
We conquer the land to help them along
And tell them their life is so wrong

In reality they steal all the riches
Take their land and rape all their bitches
Enslave their people and treat them so bad
Reading this makes me so sad

The empire is cruel I have to say
They try to excuse this in their own way
By only speaking about the best
The rest they don't mention
To hell with the rest

All empire in history has a black side too

Please read for yourself and you will see it is true

So, think of these things and all the land

If you feel greedy or want to expand

TOTALLY FREE
BY STEPHEN ROBERT SUTTON 2023

Feel the wind in your hair
Feel the sea breeze on your face
Take a day by the coast
And leave the rat race

Take a day out
On the train
On a bus or
A plane

Just to get away
Even for a day
Breathe some healthy air
And travel anywhere

Where the air is clear
And the coast is near
Just give yourself a break
And live for God's sake

Feel your feet in the sand
And hold somebody's hand
Someone that you love
See the blue skies above

Stay on the beach all night

Until the morning light

Let your love increase

I hope you all have some peace

JOURNEY'S END

by Stephen Robert Sutton 2023

Who will be with me at journey's end
Will I be greeted by a friend
Weary from travel
On a long trip
From a high mountain
Or in a dip

I carry the scars
From my own youth
And here I stand
Knowing the truth

Asking for mercy
I do sustain
Long I have lived
With all this pain

Long is the journey
Across all the sand
Pushing my body
Across the land

Shouting God have mercy
And please guide my feet
I feel that my journey

Is now complete

As arrows and spears
Pierce my skin
Attacking my body
Which so full of sin

Saying God forgive me
Let me ponder a while
Taking a breath
And giving a smile

Please stay right with me
My loyal friend
Please keep me company
Until journey's end

NOTHING IS REAL (A.I)

by Stephen Robert Sutton

From the book Nothing is real
Far beyond the reaches of the mind
Beyond reality you will find
Far beyond the credibility's of thought
To a place that is often sought

The mind creates a place so strong
Bringing all your thoughts along
Signs try to alert you but to no avail
Nothing is real and it is no tale

The signs they say nothing is real
Causing anxiety for you to feel
For life isn't real to me
So why on earth can't you see

Your life is a deception
While you look for perfection
This is an elusion
A world of confusion

Nothing is real to me
You see
Nothing is real to me
In an artificial world of intellectual life

Life goes on without any strife

But nothing is real

No nothing is real

CURSED

(from the book of the same name) by Stephen Robert Sutton 2023

Mirror, mirror on the wall
Which victim is about to fall
Whatever scares you and gives a fright
Will remain with you both day and night

Looking into the mirror with fear
The cursed souls will stay near
To plague you with all they can find
And play games with your mind

With spiders and snakes came of the mirror to you
Spitting and biting you won't know what to do
Visit the swamp and sink in the mud
Fighting the curse like you know you should

Death is waiting in dark corners you see
Fighting the curse will set you free
First you must search the origin in the past
And finally finish the curse at last

FITTING IN

By Stephen Sutton

How I really feel
I want to tell you
About my experience
It is very real

It's about fitting in
In place very strange
Meeting new people
My life rearranged

The love of my life
Comes from this place
He can see I am struggling
When he looks at my face

The loneliness
When we are apart
The isolation
Is breaking my heart

It's a constant battle
Just to fit in
In a institution
Where the walls are so thin
People can see me

But seldom lend me a hand

Busying themselves

To rule all the land

who is this about?

BY MEGAN MARPLE
REGARDING HER PARENTS' DIVORCE

Two houses, two homes, two kitchens, two phones,

Two couches where I lay, two places that I stay,

Moving, moving here and there, from Monday to Friday

I'm everywhere,

Don't get me wrong, it's not that bad

But often times it makes me sad,

I want to live that nuclear life,

With a happy dad and his loving wife,

A picket fence, a shaggy dog,

A fireplace with a burning log,

But it's not real, it's just a dream,

I cannot cry or even scream,

So here I sit with cat number three,

Life would be easy if there were two of me

SRS BOOKS

Books available by myself under various names

EIGHT SKULLS OF TEVERSHAM

CRACKED PORCELAIN

FOR THE LOVE OF CHARLOTTE

STORIES BEYOND BELIEF 1 and 2

CURSED

BLOOD TRAIL – ACROSS TIME

CONFLICT OF FAITH

UNDERSTANDING JODIE

OPERATION BRAINSTORM

DOUBLE EXPOSURE

CRACKED PORCELAIN –ACTS OF ABUSE

ADVENTURES OF THE TIME WITCHES

THE ADVENTURES OF THE TIME WITCHES

Two time travelling witches Natasha and Crystal meet up and venture across time and space in search of answers to their unique powers and the answer to the resurrection of souls.

During their adventures they meet up with the evil wizard of Zenor who threatens to destroy all witches and take away their powers for good. The witches kidnap his goblin in an effort to remain safe from his evil clutches.

From the 'Eight Skulls of Teversham –Origin of the witches